UNPACKING EMOTIONAL BAGGAGE

An Adventurous Journey to the Soul

Penny Payton

CONTENTS

INTRODUCTION

Investing in what a child finds important greatly increases their value internally as they become adults.

At the end of a long dirt road in the high desert of California, lived a family of three. The road, barely wide enough for one car, was rutted and rocky. On either side stood Joshua Trees, manzanitas, and an occasional patch of blue lupins popping up in the spring, that were home to coyote, rattle snakes, and scorpions. The land had been homesteaded by the parents of a young girl yet to be born. Together they pieced together a ramshackle structure which would become home to crushing dysfunction born out of deep ignorance.

Childhood can be unsuspectedly filled with trauma. The mind of a child is too young to cope with the pain, fear and confusion that results from many situations. For a child, without the proper tools and guidance, even the subtle moments can linger in their minds. Unless a solid foundation which teaches proper coping skills is created, the trauma will have no outlet and can become deeply hidden and cause a multitude of issues in adulthood.

The subconscious takes on the job of the protector, keeping the trauma locked away which will likely cause anxiety. Further, when children receive any type of messaging that indicates that their emotions are unimportant, moving into adulthood can become a minefield of dysfunction, terror, and/or rage. Children can internalize things that seem harmless to an adult and carry shame for years.

Harsh words, when left unprocessed or unexplained, can diminish a child's emerging sense of self. If the child is too shy, frightened, or unable to ask for help, these moments can cause them to build walls around their emotions for own their well-being. As the authenticity of the true self falls back behind those walls, a guarded version becomes the public face. From behind that face, the individual can feel less of a disappointment and be more accommodating, while seeking to become more acceptable to family and society.

I had no idea a part of myself had been emotionally shut down and no reason to even consider such a thing. Most people probably wouldn't consider it but now that I've gone through this process I'm certain everyone can benefit from taking a closer look.

I had the help of two professionals to unravel the blocks and uncover my truth. While I encourage everyone to find their own truth it's important to find help if you need it too. This book is the culmination of my research over the last ten years and the opinions I share are what this research has shown to be consistently true.

My goal initially was to lose weight. After sixty plus years of frustrating trial and error I thought it was important to share the only path that finally worked for me. I know a lot of people are looking for ways out of dysfunctional behavior. Everyone would like to be happy and at peace.

Understanding my past finally allowed me to take full responsibility and own everything I did, every single one of my actions. Which was important because no one else was going to do it for me. Too often we only look to outside sources without looking inward. I had to dig deep into the cause of my own dysfunctional behavior by looking at each specific action during the times I overate. Those actions were what led me to the false beliefs which were stored in my subconscious from childhood. Those false beliefs were what caused the anxiety that triggered the behavior of overeating. And understanding those things finally freed me from the loop of self-destructive behavior.

By uncovering the deeply hidden pain, fear and confusion and doing the work to understand, process and release it, I found self-awareness, mindfulness, inner peace, and happiness.

Even though childhood trauma is becoming m o r e of a mainstream topic, many people still cannot grasp the possibility of it existing within their own lives. I'm hoping my story will change those perspectives.

Trauma is not what you may expect, it can be very subtle and sneaky. When it occurs within a home that seemed normal, caring, or even loving, it can be impossible to imagine. But all too often it's there. Sometimes just quietly in the messaging. What may seem like gentle notes of caution or reminders from our parents can be easily be mistaken by within a child's mind, overlooked and left unprocessed, which can shape the course of our lives in ways we may not have considered.

Just for a moment, consider it for yourself. I hope you enjoy taking this adventure with me and I wish you peace, love, and happiness on your own path.

Photo: The looming shadow of darkness over my childhood innocence.

CHAPTER 1: THE LINE BETWEEN LIFESTYLES

Just when you think you have it all figured out, you find you were being an idiot all along.

In the Spring of 2012, my life ceased to exist. Not only had I come frighteningly close to death, the life I'd built was also crumbling around me. And while this took place at Easter, that old life was not to be resurrected. But it did seem to be divinely guided in a new direction.

I wasn't looking for change, my life was planned out and going as scheduled. But like the unwilling cliff diver, I suddenly found myself falling into an abyss of darkness with no idea where I would land. The cautiously cultivated illusion of control that had taken fifty-three years to construct evaporated like the morning mist. What began that Spring wound through an entire decade - turning into an intense journey - twisting its way through my past - shaking me to my core.

Change was the last thing I wanted but sometimes, when you can't see clearly enough to get out of your own way, that's exactly what's needed. Even when it looks like you are living an amazing life you can still entirely miss out on everything important, and that's what I had been doing.

There had been signs. For as long as I could remember something had gnawed at me like a barely audible chant repeating in the back of my mind. The not-so-subtle reminder that I needed to lose weight. Maybe we all have that one thing we drag around that just pisses us off. It was my nemesis that became the beacon in the darkness and the steady guide that finally moved me into a better place. For so long, I'd mistaken friend for foe.

Honestly, I'd been mistaken about a lot of things, like thinking my life had been a good one. While I'd been surrounded by privilege, I felt anything but. My time had been dedicated to the pursuit of things and experiences that I knew other people dreamed about. But I truly had no dreams of my own. I rarely felt happy. Somewhere along the way I'd jumped into the proverbial rat race and had never questioned it at all. Somehow I had bought into the belief that was the right thing to do. I lived unaware, on the surface, completely shut down to emotional awareness, all the while firmly believing I was totally aware.

And food – well food was what kept me sane as I'd bull dozed my way through life. It was an unhealthy relationship we had together, one I did not understand no matter how hard I tried. No amount of diets, gym memberships, or relationships with personal trainers brought lasting results. Oddly it would be food that would eventually lead the way out.

My old life would soon feel as if it had belonged to another person. But not before I uncovered the devastation of generation trauma which had ravaged both myself and my son.

Slowly the hidden parts of myself would emerge. I had hardly noticed that I hadn't noticed myself much at all before this all began. When had we learned to settle into the background of our own existence? And how had it happened so easily.

Climbing my way out of the deep sleep of denial and peering into emotional self-awareness was like a culture shock within my mind.

Balance, it seems, can't be found by paying attention only to things on the outside. My focus had been external. I was working harder for everyone else than I was for myself because I was taught money was security. That's what I prioritized. Over myself, over my son, over it all.

Why I thought I knew myself or cared about myself is a mystery, which should have been evident in how I treated myself personally. We seem to be conditioned to assume this stuff is an innate part of the human experience. It is not.

The truth was, I'd been taught to ignore myself in most ways. I'd been taught to ignore my emotions which left me with no idea of how to properly manage myself emotionally and with very stunted empathy. I'd been taught to ignore myself physically and to not be concerned about my future. I was taught the opposite of self-awareness. This was a walled off life void of empathy, compassion, and kindness because I was hiding my true self so I wouldn't be vulnerable again.

That false belief, the worship of money above all else is what drove me out of bed early each morning. It led me to take on the workload of five people. It pushed me to care more about the demands of everyone else and not give myself a second thought along the way. Day after day. Work had become my identity and I hadn't even noticed.

Admittedly when you are in the middle of it, it's much harder to see the truth, life just continues along like there is nothing to question. But there were things I should have been questioning. My job for example, how was it possible to run a ten-million-dollar business but not manage myself around food.

Sure, my job as the director of operations for an established fine dining group was stressful but weight had been a problem for me since birth. The job just made it easier to shove the issue farther into the background. I hadn't even been able to admit that I had an eating disorder. I saw the issue with weight as something that just needed to go away. I just wanted it to stop. I didn't think I needed to face anything. I couldn't admit it was my work to do because I had no idea what to do.

But once I became that emotional cliff diver, there was no other option than to face reality. And the truth was that somewhere rattling around in my otherwise normal-seeming brain was a sneaky parasite, one that insisted upon leading me down some dark back alleys when it came to food.

I wasn't a junkie. There were no secret stashes of candy stuffed in drawers or the ingredients for a chocolate cake hidden deep within the pantry. My kitchen was the opposite. My shiny new fridge sat empty most of the time. The cupboards held only healthy foods. Even my top-of-the-line Bosch dishwasher had stopped working from a lack of use before the warranty expired.

It may be easy to assume that people who are overweight love food, but sometimes it's the reverse. Sometimes we hate having to eat. This is why I skipped so many meals, it felt like once I opened that refrigerator door there was no closing it.

A food addiction is additionally frustrating because you cannot abstain. That makes it harder to call it an addiction or admit to it being a disorder. But there is also no hiding it, you wear it all over your body. Just walking into the grocery store caused me shame because I knew food was my boss.

The ice cream section in the frozen food isle broke me. I tried to play it off by striding right up and grabbing a big box filled with ice cream bars like I had a house full of kids. Secretly I hoped no one saw the urgency in my eyes as the box rolled up the belt toward the cashier. The sweet beeping sound as those Drumsticks were scanned began to ease my tension.

In this way I could pretend I was just buying a snack. Chips or candy could too easily be ripped open in the parking lot. But the messiness of these ice cream cones topped with nuts and hard chocolate helped me make it all the way home so I could extend my denial. And there I would sit, plopped in front of the TV opening them up, one by one.

For me this compulsion wasn't about comfort. I didn't find comfort in food, in fact being around food was anything but comfortable. What I wanted was the feeling of being soothed. And those frozen treats did the trick, as long as I kept eating until I felt better. Once I felt driven like this (triggered, the proper term I would later learn) I knew I wasn't just stopping by the store for a snack. This was a totally different type of shopping trip.

And then came the next dilemma. Somehow, maybe just to believe I was somewhat sane, I would not let myself finish an entire box. So there were leftovers. No matter how much I wanted to leave the rest in the freezer to finish the charade which had begun at the store, I knew I wouldn't make it through the night. The rest would haunt me until I ate those too.

So, to the trash bin we went, my sweet friends and me. The bin's dark, heavy void became one more limitless source of shame. Its rolling agility mocking my ever-expanding waist as it gobbled up the remains which I dropped piece by piece, just to make sure I wouldn't fish them out again. Anger rose as I slammed the lid, tears streaming down my face, vowing in desperation to never repeat this demoralizing exchange. But this twisted tirade would indeed continue and the battle between food and the bathroom scale would rage on. Unrelenting frustration leveled me, but no amount of tears, pleading or prayers made a lasting difference.

So, it was here that I turned my focus after my life had been toppled. Forced to let go of all the excuses I'd made about my weight, to admit my issue was a deeper one, an unknown malignant darkness that kept sneaking around and turning my brain into its bitch when it came to food. I was determined to find its origin because, truthfully at that time I had nothing else to do.

CHAPTER 2: PERCEPTION

Life is seen through the lens of our own personal experiences, yet somehow we expect everyone else to see it the same way too.

Most people assumed that I should have been happy with the life I had left behind because I had some amazing experiences and was making decent money. I was miserable.

Most of the time I felt like there were expectations placed on me that I had no idea how to meet. It felt like everyone assumed I should know things that I had no way of knowing. It wasn't a judgement of me personally, more like people were surprised by how I was at times. It had been that way my whole life.

Ultimately, when you are somewhat *raised by wolves* I guess that makes perfect sense. I just hadn't realized how much I resented those assumptions or how much anxiety they had added until I started thinking more about myself.

I think that perception of the grass being greener on the other side and the belief that someone needs to be happy because you believe you would be in their shoes is bullshit. If we can be honest and think about it - things like money, prestige and keeping up appearances are not required at all to be happy.

For twenty-seven years I'd dedicated myself to organizing expensive dinners, lavish parties and orchestrating all the little details that no one really thinks about as they enjoy a nice meal out. That effort paid off; the restaurants were award winning and had been featured in the pages of Vogue, Gourmet and Food & Wine.

Being surrounded by the powerful, wealthy, and privileged had skewed my perspective in some ways but the truth was, I was just the stereotypical corporate drone, unaware of how much I was risking by neglecting all other areas of my life.

I couldn't understand how I ended up there in the first place. I was just a scrappy kid from the High Desert who had become a mother far too young in life and had to pick up the pieces after a divorce in my early twenties. I was working my very first job in fast foods but knew it wasn't going to be enough to support myself and my son.

In one of the many odd twists of fate that changed my life, I was transferred to another Carl's Jr. location. This one was far busier as it was on the way to Vegas and served busloads of people at a time. And it was there someone had brought up the idea of moving to San Diego. It seemed so out of nowhere, such a strange idea, except I had been wishing I had more access to higher education than the junior colleges that were nearby.

But there was William to consider, my son who needed to be my first priority. My beautiful boy was born when I was just eighteen years old, a year after I'd graduated high school. Had I had any sense of the importance of proper priorities as a parent I would have made other decisions at that time. But coming straight out of a house where I had been an afterthought myself, I was just doing the best I could.

That house was like a dark hole of despair, a loveless place where I wasn't allowed to get a job and where going to college wasn't an option. I really don't know what they expected me to do but I think (because my parents were older) they were stuck in the mindset that women were to get married. So that's what I did. Keith and I had gotten married a month after graduation when I was just seventeen.

I know I left there filled with resentment. I wanted to prove to my parents what a loving family looked like.

I wanted to be better than them. But I had no way of knowing all the damage that had been done. Not surprisingly, the marriage with Keith failed. He put in for a transfer with the Air Force and moved to Australia. I know it killed him to leave our son behind. I will never forget how torn up he looked hugging our small child goodbye, but I was tearing up his heart in ways I had no way of understanding.

That's why the idea of this move felt like a lifeline but how could I work full time, start college courses, and raise my son? I knew no one in San Diego, so I thought it would be better to get established before I brought William along. I left him with my folks for what I believed would be a short period of time. Now, I think it was one of the stupidest things I've ever done in my life. It was just the first in a series of ways I would disappoint my son. I could not recognize I was a mom who was still a child herself. I didn't see it as my abandoning my own child. I didn't know I had been emotionally abandoned myself early on.

Off I went. San Diego may have been the biggest city I'd lived in, but back in 1984, it still had that small town vibe. That made my first time being all on my own far less scary. I had been able to transfer to another Carl's Jr. and had enrolled in classes at City College with the intention of transferring to one of the bigger schools once I'd completed all of my pre-recs.

I knew no one and loved meeting a lot of new people but this added a dimension I was not ready for - dating. In high school, I was awkward. I'd only dated two people before I met William's dad Keith in my junior year. In San Diego there were plenty of men everywhere and a lot of them seemed to be interested in me, which was a whole new exciting experience.

What I should have been doing was getting to know the area and looking for a two-bedroom place in a safe neighborhood near the beach to bring my son home to me. I could have used the energy I spent with these guys learning to surf instead. But I was too young to know that the lack of love from my parents had left me vulnerable to seeking it out in relationships. And when I needed it least, in another twists of fate, I met a man who wanted to get serious.

We wouldn't have met at all had it not been for two things; a car accident and the long wait on the police report to determine who was at fault. In fear of that responsibility, I took on a second job, which was where I met Alfred and also when I started making a lot of tradeoffs.

I'd come there to focus on school, but this man insisted I needed a better job. Since I'd learned to ignore what I wanted and focus on money as a kid I followed along without giving it any thought. I started looking for a new job. Instead of moving William home with me I moved in with Alfred.

When Keith returned to the states and was remarried William went to live with his dad and stepm o m for the school years and spent summers in San Diego. In my mind, it would be the best of both worlds for him. I believed Keith's situation was far more stable than my own and I think I was right in that.

I answered a simple want ad for an assistant to the owner position which turned into a career spanning nearly three decades. One minute I'd been leaning out the drive-thru window waiting for someone to scrape together enough change out of their ashtray to pay for their burgers and the next I was turning down dinner reservations for some of the biggest names in the entertainment industry.

Who knew I had been one job application away from arriving in the lifestyles of the rich and famous. Somehow just going to work ridiculously made me feel like I myself had arrived. In those early years that restaurant was the hot ticket in town. And I was swept up in the glamor of the fine-dining industry with Alfred nudging me along. He suggested I learn all I could at the job and before I knew it my dream of a college degree was quietly swept aside, and I was too young to know all I would miss by letting myself be carried away.

The energy of a popular restaurant is vibrant and the

kitchen was a buzz. At any given time, you might hear any one of three or four different languages coming from a wait person trying to upstage another to get what was needed for their tables.

We were fortunate to have a lot of regular guests who treated our staff like family and that was how I got lucky enough to go to an NBA playoff game! Back in the Magic Era of Showtime, when games were still being played at the Fabulous Forum and Chick (the mustard is off the hotdog) Hern was calling the plays for the Los Angeles Lakers. A friend and I bought tickets at the start of each season but not in a million years had we thought that we'd end up a few rows above Jack Nicholson's courtside perch, seated in the Laker family section during the NBA finals! As Chick would say we had our heads on a swivel!!!

Through the connections I made at this job I was having experiences that would make the most well thought out bucket lists jealous.

One day as I passed a table I noticed a SeaWorld emblem on a man's polo shirt. I'd just been there and had done something called dinner with Shamu, so I introduced myself and shared that with him. He smiled and asked how I liked it. My lame attempt at humor was to say it could have been better if Shamu had joined us at our table. The guy's smile turned curious and with a sideways glance he pulled out his business card. Handing it to me he said, "I can do one better than that". And that's how I found myself at SeaWorld at 8:00 a.m. one morning hugging Shamu in a private photo session with Sea World's official photographer.

Something similar happened years later when our second restaurant hosted a fund-raising dinner for then sitting president, Bill Clinton. The event was both thrilling and exhausting. After dealing with the secret service and the millions of details involved in planning something like this when all was set, I was ready for a break.

As I went to exit the dining room I ran face first into a wall of media which left me completely stuck and intimidated. A lovely young man who was the head of the White House Mess calmly assured me it was ok for me to be there. We quietly chatted about what he was required to do to clear the president to eat his meal. He told me that his sister had worked at that very restaurant many years back. And he invited me to visit the White House! It was one of those casual "if you are ever in D.C…" type of invites but that was not going to stop me. If he was serious, I was making the trip.

By this time, I was married to my second husband Derek and sure enough, we packed up the next month and made a visit to the Capital. We were not only treated to a private tour of the White House but also taken to the front of the line for the standard tour the next day. It was surreal to stand at the doorway of the oval office and charming to hear the first dog, Buddy bark, especially since we had a chocolate lab of our own at home.

This was the lifestyle I was living. I've been to the World Series, the Super Bowl, to restaurants with wait lists so long you have to know someone to get in. My friends and I have been hosted for annual retreats at vineyards in Napa. Presidents, celebrities, and athletes visited our restaurants regularly. From the outside, my life looked freaking awesome. How could I not be happy, right?

CHAPTER 3: WHAT WE RESIST PERSISTS

Being certain sometimes just means you are stuck.

I was at the far end of the spectrum when it came to cluelessness; if not, the powers that be wouldn't have had to try and kill me to get my attention. But that was the shock that I needed to prove I knew nothing.

While I may joke about being raised by wolves, it has crossed my mind that the wolves may have provided a better outcome. I was probably wild and rebellious enough to be part of another pack.

When this all started, when I was having to go out to my car so I wouldn't pass out at work, it would have been good if I'd known how to look inward at all.

Instead, I went to Kaiser and left pissed off because they said I needed a blood transfusion. I wasn't having it. The idea of someone else's blood running through my body sounded terrifying. I guess it my history with the medical profession, which had gone off track in the seventh grade, didn't help in this situation.

Let's just say I've had some bad breaks. The first of which came during a soft ball game in junior high. As I slid into first base the bone in my wrist shattered. The coach said it was so loud she heard it all the way in the dugout. Months later, when my first and only cast was removed, I was left with a gigantic knot because the bone had been set improperly. It still gives me problems.

Next were the awful headaches. They attached me repeatedly, right over my left eye, when William was just a toddler. At that time the doctor said it was the stress of having a one-year-old and sent me away with a bottle of aspirin. Strangely (not), the headaches continued until the day I happened to pick up a book someone left behind in the checkout line at Target. A book on food allergies.

Back in the seventies that wasn't a hot topic, I mean, we all still ate peanuts without giving it a second thought. I didn't even have to buy the book, just a quick search on headaches showed me the culprit was chocolate. I suppose indirectly the doctor had been right, I'd been eating the chocolate because I was stressed! But cutting it out stopped the headaches.

While food has been my nemesis in many ways, over time it has also become a guiding light. Before heavily processed items became a questionable food source, those allergies had already taught me to pay good attention to ingredient lists because of my body's reaction. I have been able to match up aches and pains with inflammation stemming from processed junk food, white flour, white sugar, and various sources of proteins. My legs get restless when I eat salt. I've had an ocular migraine from too much red wine, swollen lips from too much avocado and headaches because of both chocolate and corn. I've had such bad pain I've gotten x-rays only to find it was a certain type of protein bar causing the issue.

In the early 90's, in another fluke of sorts, I became a vegetarian because of live animal overload! That was the year my husband Derek and I got annual passes for SeaWorld and the zoo, brought home our goofy chocolate lab, Flap and the year we packed everyone up in an RV for a road trip.

That trip became the tipping point. William had taken the dog for a stroll, and I happened along just as Flap was nose to nose with a cow they'd met. I snapped a shot and after one look at that photo I said, "I don't want to eat either of those guys", and I was done with all animal consumption.

Somehow by the grace of all that's good I've come a long way from the little girl who got shamed on the rare trips to the dentist for eating too much candy and who used to have meat and potatoes with every meal!

Unfortunately, none of that helped with the exhaustion I had been suffering. So, there I went the next day, back to the same doctor, who was clearly fighting a losing battle to not roll his eyes at me.

Assessing my appearance and glancing at the latest test results, he began to speak in a much more urgent tone than that of the previous day. With frank certainty, he assured me that getting a blood transfusion immediately was one of only two options. And the second was very grim. If I refused again, in a few short hours my organs would shut down one by one, and I would be dead before the end of the day. Well Fuck. All of a sudden getting a blood transfusion was the least terrifying option I had.

It's quite shocking to face your own death like that, especially when it has not crossed your mind at all. And I almost let it happen. I could have easily gone home from work and went to sleep and not woken up again.

The culprit had been my own body...or rather my own stupidity. But here's the thing, I should have known. I'd been having a terrible time with my period as I'd gotten older and had been losing a lot of blood. I mean a lot of blood. I just thought it was a natural thing, a normal part of aging.

On a good day, this visit would have been the end of the

story. But no, I took this time as another opportunity to prove just how unaware I was and how little self-care mattered to me. In one day, I had learned I was near death, got two units of blood and then got up and went right back to work. Who goes right back to work after a day like this? A fucking work consumed idiot, that's who.

I wanted to blame the hospital staff for assuming I would know what to do but in truth I was the poster child for the necessity of disclaimers. This was what had followed me through life, that expectation from others that I should know things I had no way of knowing. It wasn't like I'd been in a situation like this before. I cannot stress enough that self-love is not innate and the ability to self-care is not a given either. With a smile and a wave, they wished me well and sent me on my way. Maybe that's the reason for those follow-up appointments, to check up on dumbass's like me.

The next day I squared off again with Dr. Eyeroll, who came through the door looking very pissed off. My hemoglobin count, which began at what I learned was a horrifically low number of 5, hadn't climbed to the anticipated level. It hadn't even inched up to a 6 count yet.

With a pace far too brisk for the square footage we occupied, Dr. Eyeroll headed toward the chair behind his desk, and with sincere kindness in his eyes, asked me what I had been doing. As he began to take a seat, I said, "nothing really, just going to work".

For a moment I thought Dr. E was going to miss his chair completely and land on the floor. The bottom of my chart clanged loudly on the top of his desk as the kindness dissipated in his eyes. His mouth had fallen wide open. With a shake of his head, he lifted the handset of his desk phone. I wondered if he was considering calling for a psych hold. Instead, he asked for the number of my employer. This tall, salt and pepper haired man seemed desperate to gain some form of control over a situation that was rapidly circling the drain.

My shoulders slumped. Dr. E. explained the proper course of action would have been for me to have gone home and rest. In other words, to take care of myself and forget about work. Now he was insisting that I take at least five full days off and he was ready to call my boss to make sure I did.

A deep and familiar sense of humiliation rose from the pit of my stomach, bringing with it the first color my cheeks had seen in days. My chin dropped to my chest, sucking dry the last of my energy.

This pattern, running its course like a brook snaking through the woods at dusk, had been sneaking up on me from the dark corners of my life for as long as I could remember. It stayed there waiting, wanting to burble up like rushing water confronting a boulder as it made its way down stream. One day I would understand where and how this all had begun, but until then the shame of now knowing how to do better for myself remained.

CHAPTER 4:
JUST DOING THE BEST WE CAN

We all do our best with what we have but that does not excuse the pain we cause along the way.

Shame tended to follow me around since my first memories of grade school. I started a half a year late because parenting seemed to be an afterthought in my family. That tardiness made me the new kid in the class and my school photos all show the terror in my eyes, kind of like the look on a dog's face who's new to the dog park and lacks socialization. Panic and confusion became my newest companions.

It wasn't that my mom intended for me to have that start to my education, she was like most, just doing the best she could with what she had to work with. But that doesn't make the pain of my parent's ignorance any less devastatingly real, just like the pain I caused my own child. That trickle-down effect is what makes trauma generational and causes us to overcompensate with our own kids. We may mean well, but if we haven't made peace from within, we can still cause long, lingering damage.

This is why I'm not a fan of intentions, not even the kind meant for manifestation, because I've found within the flow of consciousness, your desires can be known without having to set an intention around them. And even the best intended humans can cause a huge amount of damage.

On that first day of class I showed up to Mrs. Brown's kindergarten class with an untied shoelace and no idea how to fix the situation. In stepped the boy who would become my true north, Jeff, the teacher's son. He stepped right up and helped me with my shoe issue. And we became destined to go all the way through high school calling each other brother and sister, dating each other's friends, going to school dances, and being there for the best and worst of times. Mrs. Brown and I would go on to exchange Christmas cards until she reached her 90's. Jeff, would sadly pass way far too young and leave a life-sized hole in my heart.

Unfortunately, the rest of the teachers and students were not like the Browns and those years in elementary school had scarred me the deepest because my home life shined right on through to the classrooms.

In first grade kids started asking me why my hair was so ratty. I had to force my mom to brush my hair which she agreed to as long as I kept the pain of her pulling it to myself. Why hadn't I been taught any self-grooming by then? The kids also wanted to know why I smelled so much like smoke. I didn't know it was because both of my parents were chain smokers. At that age that was my own personal version of normal.

But when it came to my weight it wasn't the kids who tormented me. It started with Mrs. McEanery, the stern, dark-haired woman who had been entrusted with the first graders back in 1964.

She had taken it upon herself to collect stories about her students' lives and took the time to print them as keepsakes from our youth. I hung onto those pages for years, right along with the feelings welled up inside because of them. I still remember the day she passed them out to us. As the other kids were getting glowing remarks and kind comments my anticipation had grown. She had neared my desk. Finally, she stood right beside me, her black pencil skirt brushing my desk as she leaned in my direction. I waited with pride, knowing she would have something great to say about me and my stories too.

She glanced to the side, not facing me, smirking. She began to shake her head as she spoke, asking why the only thing I had to talk about was food. Leafing through the pages, she commented on every meal that had been captured within the large font type she'd used. She stopped, taking the time to look at me, and dropped the paper on my desk. The rest of the class roared with laughter at the only chubby kid who had nothing better to do but talk about what she ate. Years later, once I realized how abusive that was, those fucking papers went straight into the trash can.

Blaming an innocent child for something they have no responsibility for or control over is not just unkind, it is cruel. Isn't it common sense to think that if a child has nothing better to talk about than mealtime she likely won't have the emotional support at home to process abuse at school? It would be great if, all these years later public shaming like that and personally humiliating someone was a thing of the past. But here we are decades later, and it's only gotten worse. Now it seems, some want to normalize it.

We are caught up in a loop that has been perpetuated for a long while and prioritizing money over humanity and family had been a large contributor. As long as we are taught to ignore our inner selves and lack the basic foundation to manage our own emotions it will continue. We step into adulthood seeking whatever we were missing at home and that's what drives our lives, creates our dysfunction, and causes the use of addiction and distraction as avoidant coping - or at least this is what my experiences have proven to be true.

A part of me shut down that day in first grade. I gradually became a combination of the dopey kid who ignored insults and the strong kid no one wanted to mess with. I imagine how different it would have been had I been taught to pay attention to how I felt as young child. Assuming a child is ready for adulthood without assuring they can manage their own emotions is a recipe for failure and I was the poster child.

Photo: Me in first grade.

For so long a library-sized collection of shame sat on my internal bookshelf because neglect had filled the gaping holes where love should have been in my early life.

I think of the families we see on film. Two adults who love each other so much that they want to share that love by creating their own family. But when you subtract the love, add in neglect and sprinkle criticism on top, ladies, and gentlemen, we have ourselves a recipe for dysfunction. Instead of being wrapped in a warm blanket of love, acceptance, and security I learned to wrap myself up in a protective layer of fat. Which was to remain my guardian until I finally felt safe enough to peek out all by myself.

So, just like that first day of school, I still felt clueless when I saw the look on Dr. Eyeroll's face - the familiar pain of letting someone down without really understanding why. We agreed that I would stay at home and rest the five days. What would happen at work would just have to happen. And boy, did things happen.

CHAPTER 5: SOME GOODBYES ARE LONG OVERDUE

Unraveling a false sense of security.

Those first few days were lost entirely to sleep. I did nothing – like nothing. I doubt that I ate or showered. The last thing I wanted to do was talk to anyone, especially someone from work but I did take one call from my assistant Mick who was in absolute panic about a mistake he'd made. Even though I was on medical leave and couldn't be expected to work, I wanted to help. I just didn't have the strength or presence of mind to do so.

Five days passed with the speed of five minutes. That last night, as I was out gingerly navigating the sidewalks of my suburban neighborhood, hoping to generate some energy, my boss called. With each 70s-style home I passed, every manicured yard started to look more like a cozy place to curl up and go back to sleep. I listened as he assured me we were family, said he hoped I felt better, and would be happy that I'd be back in the morning. I guessed they'd figured out whatever issues Mick had been having but the next day, the slow burn of reality burbled up through the chaos.

Following Dr. E's orders by completely ignoring work and stepping up my own self-care left me again unprepared. In time I did finally review the messages, dozens of them, each more brutally intense that the last. But before I'd even had time to talk to my assistant, the owner had was on the phone wondering if Mick had been fired yet. I couldn't wrap my head around what he was saying so he asked to speak to Mick and just fired him on the spot. My heart pounded as the heat of humiliation rose to scorch my ears.

Together we'd dedicated thirty-five years to the place, and we were both flabbergasted. Apparently a mistake Mick had made with the Easter menus and his attempt to correct it were the grounds. In that moment, all I saw was the pain and humiliation on Mick's face. While he'd been given a week to find another job, I understood why he couldn't stand to be there one more second. He was right. I was heartbroken and devastated but he was right. So now what? My energy had not returned to work with me yet somehow it was expected that I could double my workload. When I told the owner I couldn't do it his reply was that I'd have to "figure it out". I knew I couldn't do it and said as much.

So, there I was, the person I'd counted on to help me recover my mojo at work had just walked out the door because the person who said I was family just the night before had apparently turned his back on us both.

There wasn't room for conversation. There was nowhere else to turn so I called HR, a couple who worked as outside consultants. I'd spoken to them countless times before and I had hoped they could talk me through this. They did try to help, but in the end, this time they were not there to be my ally. If I was leaving they wanted to know if I could give my notice in writing. I hadn't actually wanted to give notice. I was just not physically in shape to take on Mick's work too.

Two weeks later I was gone and the reality of how it all happened took far longer to process. The owner had mistakenly thought I had been following all of the communication when instead I had been asleep, so it was all a matter of miscommunication.

It would turn out to be the best thing for all involved. At the time it sucked. In less than three minutes time two lives had been annihilated. Execution via phone. Any sense of security, and even a little of my own faith in humanity was lost.

Sometimes it seems like things were set up in a way so that I'd have no choice but to leave. And now I'm sure there was more involved than just the divine conspiring to make it happen. Either way, I was stuck at the absolute lowest point in my life with no other option, feeling cast aside, like my effort had meant nothing at all.

CHAPTER 6: LOST IN WHO I THOUGHT I WAS

Our true selves are in there, clawing their way out from under the garbage of denial.

A part of me knew I wasn't meant to stay there as long as I had because I'd tried to quit a dozen times over the years. But the way things happened had been so shocking and felt so unjust it left me very indignant at first. Eventually I'd find gratitude. The time has served me well even though the ending could have been much more kind.

Again, the self-care involved in processing this internal pain was not high on the priority list. Money was. The fear of insecurity reared its ugly head, and I focused on finding another job right away. Friends and people that I'd known from work assured me I would be snapped up right away and when I wasn't...well I nearly snapped.

Hope sprang with each ring of the phone, like a bell tolling for my next voyage to begin and faded as no job offers came my way. Wave after wave of self-pity washed me back onto the lonely shore of emptiness, my identity eroding like the sand flowing out to the sea. I had nothing to do, nowhere to be, no need to set an alarm and none of it had been my choice. Not one single thing.

The dearest and bravest of friends who chose to keep me close were calling to check in, and patiently helping me wrestle the giant dumpster fire of emotions I'd landed in. And when shame rose at the idea of taking unemployment, one of them brilliantly reminded me how I'd paid into that fund for decades. My resume had been polished, I kept applying faithfully but no one had been interested. I had been near the top of my industry but was suddenly finding myself un-hirable.

Money dominated my thoughts more now than ever before. Silently I wondered if God was laughing at the plan I'd had to have my house paid off within the next three years. Fortunately, a quick mortgage refi helped, but with zero job prospects, by the time the benefits ended, this lifestyle would be unsustainable. I had no idea what to do and neither did anyone else.

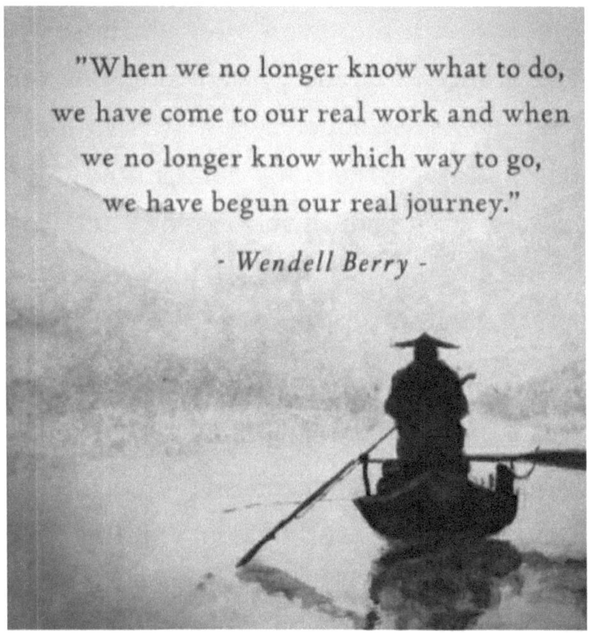

So, this was how I came to have so much time on my hands. After a few months of facing how hurt I felt by shouting, crying and making multiple trips to get ice cream, I finally began to get a grip. Once the panic settled I was able to assess things more realistically. I was being given a chance to question a lot of things and that was how I finally realized I hadn't taken much time to really look at what I wanted in life. Between looking for money and love I'd left myself far over to the side. And the funny thing I would learn was that those things, money, and love are far better when you don't seek them out so aggressively.

Wanting things as a kid had not worked out well for me

and that stuck with me. Even after all those years and having the ability to choose, I had not. The only thing I'd ever let myself seriously want was to lose weight, which also hadn't worked out. That's how my nemesis launched me onto a path of self-exploration. It was time to deconstruct what I'd done with all the time I'd spent forging my way, unquestioning.

I started with the small things, and right away I noticed that I sure had a lot of stuff around me. It's weird to think of this as one of those light bulb moments, like maybe I'd not stopped to look around before, and the truth was, I hadn't.

I had let myself get caught up in a lot of things that didn't matter at all. There I was, in a house with three bedrooms, two bathrooms, a bonus room, a two-car garage, and a huge outdoor patio, all nestled on a large corner peninsula lot (meaning a neighboring house on only one side) *living by myself.* I mean, it was amazing...there was a crafting room with one of those fabulous project tables I'd drooled over in the Crate & Barrel catalog. I hadn't used it even once. When the girls came by for a crafting day, we worked in the dining room. I'd been so excited when I found that project table. The catalog price tag, about six- hundred bucks had scared me away, but I found it at a garage sale for a measly thirty-five bucks. I had to have it but now I was wondering why.

The second spare bedroom was outfitted as an office with a swanky Pier 1 white slatted desk, chair, and cabinet used as a printer stand. Only rarely did I leave my laptop in there to work. The master suite had a gorgeous Pottery Barn windowed buffet cabinet just to hold my collection of handbags. A magnificent ebony Z Gallery sleigh bed sat next to a matching dresser filled with clothes I doubt I'd worn twice.

At heart, I'm a very simple girl who lives in jeans, shorts, t-shirts, and flip flops. How had this happened? Labels hadn't held any appeal when it came to clothing because I didn't want attention drawn to my body. And I wasn't really all that much of a spender, so I had no idea why I had spent so much time and money on the things in my house. Had that shopping had been done to make up for something else...had I been a victim of retail therapy?

CHAPTER 7: CLEARING THE WAY

As we begin to know ourselves inwardly, outwardly things become far less important.

I have been blessed with a very lovely, kind, and amazing set of friends, each exceptionally more like family, which was great considering how little family I have. From completely supporting my emotional insanity at the beginning of this fiasco, almost each one of them had now migrated into a different camp, a camp that was devoted to questioning what I was doing with my time and what I was going to do about work.

For the first time it had become undeniably apparent to me just exactly how work-orientated our society is. It was about more than just getting up and going to work to make a living. In fact, at a certain point, it seemed to weigh far heavier on the minds of my friends than my own. I had resigned myself to not having an answer and had almost surrendered it all to fate. Maybe what I was seeing in them was something like herd mentality? Perhaps they'd been thinking when one of their own cuts from the pack, what will become of the rest? One friend, visibly shaken had said, "You're the most stable of us all", like there was a fear it would be contagious.

So, when the great purge of 2013 began, everyone panicked. I started small; first it was just one garage sale. As I rambled around in my big house I was amassing a pile of things to be set out on the driveway for bargain hunters to rifle through, early on a Saturday morning. At least now one thing was sure, I was making money again. One dollar at a time, but it was income!

The more the space opened up around me, the more I wanted to clear things out. It was like peeling the layers of an onion. I'd feel certain there was nothing else I could part with, only to start piling up more stuff to go out the door. One garage sale had me hooked. Bigger pieces, like the project table, were coming into question now. And my friends questioned my sanity, asking why I'd sell my things when I'd just need to buy them all over again. What was happening to me wasn't yet clear, but I was being led in a different direction, away from possessions, less needy of accomplishment and starting to understand money in some very different ways.

It hadn't been that long ago that my friend Katie and I had put together the cute little table and stools that sat in the middle of my kitchen. But I added it to the list of things for sale anyway. Stuff was coming out of closets, boxes were being lowered from rafters in the garage, nothing avoided my newfound scrutinizing eye for salesmanship. I shunned no platform; Craigslist, eBay, Offer Up, and garage sales had suddenly become my new at home employment gigs. After the long shitty months before this, I felt a renewed sense of purpose even though there was no real plan in place.

Back in 1993 I'd found myself doing something similar on a hot summer day the August my mom had passed away. My son William and I had found her there in her home. From the condition my guess would be that she'd passed a few days before. The one thing that I'm certain of is how poorly I handled this, like most things, with my son. I'm sure we talked about what happened but I'm equally as sure we didn't talk about how he felt about what happened. There's no doubt my focus was more on what needed to be done with all the stuff she and my dad had left behind. If nothing, I was efficient.

My dad had lived with the remnants of fear many depression era people suffered. He didn't get rid of many things. In fact, he was the guy who'd take the trash to the dump and come back with more than he'd left with. Husband Derek and one of his friends joined William and

I, there in the high desert to start clearing the decks. We had rented the biggest possible U-Haul in anticipation of making a king-sized donation. There were few memories I cherished from my time with my parents which meant there was very little that I wanted. My son found several things which he still has today. We found a couple of guns which reminded me of our friend Chuck. He was one of the only people I'd known who'd ever set foot in this God-forsaken geographical nightmare of a town. I stashed those in the car for him but was a bit deflated when he thanked me for what he called a "20-gauge squirrel gun" but hey, a gift's a gift, no backsies!

We filled up the truck and were fortunate this was back in the days when Goodwill was grateful for such a haul. Somewhere in the world is a miniature half toilet seat inspiringly decorated with the words "For my half-assed friend" and I'm okay with not knowing where that landed. Chuck, however, became one of my most trusted and faithful friends on the journey of writing this book, although I'm still not sure what he did with the squirrel gun.

The emotions surrounding that day's events were the usual emotions I felt about my parents, a deep sense of frustration. We found ourselves digging through a ridiculous historical accounting of their lives, utility receipts dating fifty years in the past, stamps torn off the corner of envelopes as if they were a collection of some sort, ID badges from the merchant marines dating back to the 1940s. A mismatch of conflicting and confused China and stoneware patterns. Jar after jar of pennies my dad had called one-centers thinking they'd be of more value at some later date. Cardboard barrels as tall as three feet and as wide as two were stuffed with non-sense paperwork that had been carted around from place to place and stored for over half a century. By the time we came to a stopping point we were all smudged with grime, grubby, and exhausted.

Mom had taken to writing in the inside covers of her books, beautiful love notes for her daughter – for me. She wrote about how I'd never know just how much she loved me, and I knew she was right, I didn't. I will remember her as the mom who was mean to me as a kid. Even keeping a few of those books has not helped, in fact, there was one book she had by Edgar Cayce I find myself wishing I had, because it would have come in handier than the others. This does help me to understand more how I feel about William. I too think he may never understand how sincere and deeply my love is for him either. But I keep trying; I desperately keep trying.

CHAPTER 8: TWELVE STEPS TO THE GYM

Comfort zones are for wimps.

Having secured this new sales gig around the house, my nerves were far less rattled. I had a bit of a path lined up at least, which opened up some space in my brain to get back to the work I needed to be doing on myself. Like the weight thing...which needed a bit of research. Grabbing my laptop and a craft beer from a local brewery, which San Diego has an ample supply of, I took a seat out on the patio and dug in.

The dramatic encounters with the big black trash can had become a bit less epic, but they were still a part of my life on a weekly basis. And if this was the one thing I really wanted in life then I needed to be committed. The first thing I did was to sign up for a 12-week course at Kaiser going by the name of "Food Addiction."

The classroom was filled with about fifteen curious souls and our leader, who was a kind and quirky guy named Steve. He had been learning about how food affects health for decades, and much like myself, had his own doubts about the medical profession which had prompted his queries! A kindred soul!

As he shared his story I had to smile. Years back Steve had been diagnosed with high cholesterol. When the medication made him feel far worse or to use his words, like dog crap, he started his research. He dumped the meds, earned an MBA in nutrition, and now stood before us to talk about how food was addicting and back then, it was not your everyday topic. It was intriguing.

As the weeks wound down, we'd shared a few things, learned a few things and at one point, to my surprise, someone had even called me insightful for the first time! I graduated from our little course feeling strong and resilient. But a few weeks later I was still there matching wits with that fucking trash can all over again... and losing.

That course was a springboard. It was validation that a large part of the food industry was working directly against the health of the public for one reason - profit. The course was an introduction into the complexity of the problem I wanted to solve. It would take me a while to come to that understanding. That is a very big part of the issue with change in a society that thrives on instant gratification. We lack the patience to dive in and swim all the way back up to the surface.

The problem with having a weight problem is – well - a big one. No one seemed to know the answer. A friend who swore by AA told me to try the "food one," which was unappealingly known as Overeaters Anonymous. Since there was no option to abstain from food I was fascinated in learning how that might work. Would I be calling my sponsor on my dreaded march out to dispose of my half-eaten pack of Drumsticks? I guess the idea would be to reach out on the way to the store, but if I couldn't pull my own head out of a deep dive into that freezer section how could a stranger convince me? Once that switch was turned on for whatever mysterious reason there was no turning it off for me.

Part of the problem in addressing anything like this is the labeling. At that point, some may have said I was a compulsive binge eater, which didn't resonate with me because I wasn't a compulsive person in any other part of my life. But without the label of a disease or a disorder how can we invite Big Pharma in to save the day right, so I get it. I just wasn't on board with those bitches. I was going in! I didn't want an outside fix.

It seemed like my own brain was hijacking me and since it was happening in my brain I wanted to find a way to fix it without the use of chemicals, if at all possible. If I were to add a label it would be one I'd made up myself, SOS. Survival Override Syndrome - because it truly seems like our brains are stuck back in the survival mode of scared children who've had no opportunity to heal the hidden pain. And when it's triggered our brains override all else to stop that pain from hurting us all over again.

I had resolved to give this next possibility the appropriate attention, so with hope and positivity I arrived at my first Overeaters Anonymous meeting. An enormous smile on my face and an unbiased mind, I was ready for all the possibilities awaiting me.

Sliding quietly into the first open chair I saw; I glanced around at the crowd. My heart dropped just a tad noticing a harsh truth - I was the smallest person in the group, something I can rarely take credit for. Oddly, I felt defeated! My attitude deteriorated a bit when not one smile was returned. I had to wonder, is it possible to feel judged for being less big?

It seemed so, yes. The stolen glances representing reverse discrimination were creeping into my psyche during those first moments. Size, whether it be reflected in the number on the tag of a piece of clothing or the extra berth it takes to clear the casing on a door, matters when you carry extra weight. Feeling small in a room filled with people who wanted nothing more in life than to be smaller didn't make me feel better about my size. I was uncomfortable in the place I'd come looking for solace.

I looked down at my flip-flop clad toes, pulling my feet back under me, thinking I'd raise my ass right out of that chair and carry it right through that door. But how would that help. I was positive it wouldn't make the group feel great either. So, there I sat, feeling like an outsider.

A woman (who must have honed her compassion over a lifetime of hard knocks) took the lead as the meeting commenced with the serenity prayer which was followed by the introductions. Then the sharing began. I took a chance and glanced around. The walls displayed the program outlines and for the first time I noticed more about the individuals, we were a group of about a dozen or so, all women. Each of the ladies were taking their turns to open a window into their personal, guilt-ridden biographies, for all to hear. When it came to my turn, I weakly offered a smile and turned to pass the baton to the next despondent soul to my right.

I was out of my league. I had nothing even remotely close to the excruciating details which had been shared within the confines of these walls. Which actually made me feel worse. Almost as if I had no reason for being overweight. I suddenly felt like a fraud in my own life.

As the meeting wrapped up we all made our way over to the refreshment table, interestingly covered with sugary treats. I began an inquisition. I had to know how long these women had been attending meetings like this. I was shocked. I should add, by this point, I'd yet to unearth my own empathy, so even though I saw the pain and sadness that bled through their eyes, all I felt was distraught. For most, it wasn't a matter of years, it had become decades of attendance. I was in a room full of women who'd resigned to live just like I was feeling in that moment, distraught. I felt defeated. As I left, they said they hoped to see me at the next meeting.

As I shut the door to my 4Runner I let my head fall back onto the headrest and closed my eyes. Breathe. I could not let this become my life. Breathe. I could not return to this meeting or any like it, not tomorrow, not this week, not ever again in this lifetime. Breathe, just keep breathing, there has to be more to life than this. I felt a renewed passion to get to the bottom of what happened to people like us and obviously it was going to take a lot of determination to find some real answers.

With nothing else to do, I carried my somewhat smaller ass over to the YMCA and signed up the next morning to work with a trainer because I had to do something that felt positive.

Drifting off to sleep that night, my logical brain knew I was miles away from the truth, but I needed a better next step if I were to survive and stay off what looked like a twelve-step road to overeater's hell. No offense to those that find solace in these programs because I get it. I really do. It just wasn't for me.

CHAPTER 9: THE IMPORTANCE OF LISTENING TO YOUR CHILDREN

Be worthy of your child's trust because they completely depend upon it.

Joining a gym felt a little like the old version of normal. The idea that exercise and diet was all it took for a healthy body felt like an escape into a world I had longed to fit into. A world that had been out of reach for a lifetime. Other than the fact that exercise had zero meaning to me. It seemed absolutely pointless. Why? When you didn't have to do it, why? And I knew more was needed. But it was a positive step to somewhere in a time I needed to get moving.

Like most things, I'd never stopped to think about why didn't I enjoy exercise. When I was young I was interested. Like in sixth grade. All year long we waited for the pool party to be held at the community center for our graduation. After all, we were moving on to junior high and leaving behind our very first school; we wanted to cut loose! Naturally, I wanted to learn to swim for the party but none of my friends had a pool or access to one either.

The closest I'd come had been joining Girl Scouts but some of those experiences seemed to lead to more embarrassment than good. We once all went on a group bike ride. Imagine my bike...a collection of scrap parts my dad had drug home from the dump. It had taken him so long to cobble it together I'd outgrown it.

As I huffed and puffed, the hot sun beaming down upon my chubby body, one of the leaders stopped me, saying we needed to turn back. I wouldn't be able to make the trip like that. So, there we were, waiting back at the starting point for my mom to pick me up. Hot tears streaking my red cheeks. I don't know if the other girls laughed at me or talked behind my back. It didn't matter, I felt horrible either way.

Dad really tried hard to come off like the guy with all the answers. He said he'd teach me to swim. He seemed to enjoy telling the stories of how he'd swam five miles in the Pacific Ocean every day when he'd lived in Long Beach. As the pudgy little girl trapped and lonely at the end of that dirt road surrounded by Joshua trees, swimming in the ocean sounded like an enormous adventure.

Considering the excitement in his eyes as he talked of those times, I was sure I'd be learning to swim. But as the weeks passed and the party drew near, not one swimming lesson had come my way. As every single one of my classmates splashed around having fun, there I sat, in all my chub glory, at the side of the pool. I sat looking on until I finally had to stumble to a shady spot where our teacher found me passed out from a sun stroke. To this day I can't be in strong sun or heat for extended periods of time. My shoulders still have huge freckles as a reminder. I actually didn't learn to swim until I was in my late twenties and, yes, that sucked as much as it sounds like it would.

It wouldn't be until high school that I would find a love for sports again. I was tall, which made basketball and volleyball both fun and exciting. But tennis was my passion and I desperately wanted to join the tennis team. I loved it so much I was excited again. Even after the swim fiasco, even after my dad vetoed my interest in band during junior high when I'd longed for a clarinet. I was really good at tennis! So good that our tiny PE teacher, Ms. Morgan had asked me to join the team. For the VERY FIRST TIME IN MY LIFE someone wanted to include me in a physical activity, and I was stoked! It just had to be possible.

That could have been where I took my very first step towards building my own life outside parental control and restriction. A step built on my own athleticism and the recognition of my abilities. Just that one small thing would have been life changing for me. But, as usual, my father wouldn't allow me the opportunity.

The shadow over exercise was cemented with a mix of deep resentment. Week after week, my dad sat in the backyard by himself as the tennis team competed at my high school and traveled for away games. Games I could have been a part of, building confidence, gaining strength, starting friendships. Would it have been so hard for him to allow this? It's no wonder I learned to dislike exercise.

My childhood was controlled and very limited. Driving the family car to school was allowed. But nothing more. Getting a job and car of my own was not allowed. This is the subtlety of trauma, the constant messages which made me feel like an unwanted burden who was just in the way.

Lack of encouragement and celebration in our lives as children can shatter our spirit for a lifetime, which was something I became aware of far too late in my own parenting. When things are important to our children, it's our duty to listen and hear with an open mind. It's important that children feel they can talk to their parents about anything without the fear of judgement or criticism because this is how they learn to accept and love themselves. It's important that there is a gradual shift allowing them the appropriate control over their own lives as they grow. If not, they can end up like me, figuring it out in their fifties.

Maybe I was just faking it by joining the Y or maybe the defeated tennis player in me still held hope for a better outcome. But, at least for a brief moment, my old normal seemed possible again. I was even opening my mind to the possibility of renting out a room on Airbnb or perhaps building an addition on my property for income.

Photo: My family.

MAR • 68

CHAPTER 10: FAMILY TIES

Generational trauma is like a subtle timebomb.

By this point I wasn't deep enough into my own issues, so William and I were still able to talk about most everything. I thought of us as very close and that having a smaller age difference had played in our favor. We had become more out of sync than I knew, primarily because I wasn't paying enough of the right kind of attention.

His life had been filled with back-and-forth flights from Seattle to San Diego, which he seemed to master like a champ from such a young age. Summer was our time and I thought we made the best of it. Unfortunately, I wasn't aware or compassionate enough to ask how he felt about the whole thing.

The summer between William's junior and senior year before he went off to college, was filled with change. He had his first serious girlfriend and naturally wanted to spend time with her instead of me. But I insisted he visit me, and this was the year we found his grandmother dead. The year I'd gotten remarried and not invited my mom to the wedding, the year we got a dog, the year we took an RV trip, the year we bought a house and remodeled it (which I demanded he help with). And the year I called him selfish, him not his actions, because he naturally did not want to help. And of course, I did not talk to him about his role amid all of this change. Just as he was at the age to find his own agency, I prevented it. I believe my poor parenting that summer changed his trajectory. That was when he first started to have noticeable changes in his weight.

I did the same thing that my parents did to me, without even knowing it. At that time, I was only able to see if from my perspective. If I had known my own empathy had been locked away when I closed off my own emotions at a young age, this would not have happened the way it did.

I saw this as our last summer together before he went off to college and things changed forever. Because I didn't know how to process my own feelings in high school, I hadn't reconciled the pain of my own desires being crushed. That too, was swept under the rug.

William should have been able to do what he wanted. Just like I should have been able to do what I wanted at that age. But since no one had cared one bit about what I'd wanted in high school, I then failed to consider what my son had wanted. He was coming into his own and this was where that gradual shift in power was so important. These are the times when they should be having their own fun and learning from their own mistakes in the safety of home with accepting and loving parents. Just as tennis would have changed my life, I firmly believe this would have changed his.

I think being denied everything I wanted so consistently as a kid played a big role in how I felt at that time. I may have even had a lot of narcissistic tendencies then. I thought William would never look back, that he'd never really want to spend time with me again. Because I hadn't wanted to spend time with my parents after I left home. He'd have the rest of his life for girlfriends, friends, and fun. And this was the picture I had for him, to enjoy his life in ways I'd not been able to. What I didn't know at that time was the divorce and his splitting his time between homes had caused him to worry deeply about how we felt. A lot of his time was spent making sure we were ok, because we felt so back each time he left. My doing this to him that summer seemed to almost cement him into that mindset.

I made him come spend that summer with me and that summer was filled with change. Along with being forced to do the opposite of what he wanted, we found his grandmother had passed away, I'd gotten married to Derek, bought a new house, added our chocolate lab Flap to the family and took the RV trip where I decided to become a vegetarian. There was too much change and not a lot of open-minded discussion about how those changes were affecting William and his place in all of the change.

To make things even worse, Derek and I were very committed to renovating our new home. I remember being so proud that we had been able to get a pool specifically because I knew William would love it. But instead of enjoying that summer we kept working on the house and I expected my son to be as excited as I was to have this home. I guess I was still trying so hard to create that family, that sense of a great home for his last summer I made it a horrible one instead.

I was far too focused on getting things done to even notice how unhappy my son was. He was being forced to do yard work and he didn't like it; at one point I even called him selfish for not wanting to improve his new home with us. What a fool I was. William would tell me one day how much my calling him selfish had hurt and that it had really messed him up. That whole summer I imagine the messaging he picked up was that what he wanted didn't matter, he wasn't first anymore, and his feelings didn't matter. It was only after years of my own intense work that I could feel how painful all of this was for him. When we carry our own pain we are so blinded to the pain we inflict upon our own children. It seems like we can block out the possibility of pain even being associated with events that have brought us pain because it's all so repressed and hidden. It's the worst form of generational trauma. It's a hideous circle of not understanding our own emotions enough to process and release them, and then imposing the exact same situations onto our children, who have also not been taught to manage how they feel. It's a grotesque loop we all need to understand and eliminate.

How could I have known when I became a mom to my beautiful child at just eighteen? I was newly married, freshly stepping out of my own hellish adolescence, and unfortunately even less ready for parenting than I had been for adulting. That made it much harder to take responsibility or blame for my behaviors because I had no idea where they'd even come from. There had been no way to rebel living there at the end of a dirt road in the middle of nowhere with no neighbors or transportation. My life was filled with ugliness. Beauty could not even be found in the nature which was filled with Joshua trees, scorpions, coyotes, and snakes.

It wasn't until I turned sixteen that my parents moved us to a house on a real paved street with people living nearby, a neighborhood of sorts. It was there, one hot desert day with temperatures in the hundreds, just a year later that my father and I stood on the crumbling driveway.

He squared his shoulders and solemnly handed me a thousand dollars in cash. My seventeen-year-old eyes were wide with confusion; money was not something my dad gave to anyone unless he absolutely had to. This was an obligation, twofold in its effort.

I was getting married to Keith, William's father, and our wedding would be a few months after my high school graduation, just before my eighteenth birthday. This was my dad's way of paying for our wedding.

As I gripped the money, just before turning away from me he said, "Now that you are turning 18, I'm no longer responsible for you." My mouth dropped wide open as I stood there with tears dripping onto the concrete, feeling embarrassed to be alive. Any chance for a sense of happiness, love or joy gone.

This is the sneakiness of generational trauma. Those moments in that driveway would play heavily in my son's transformation into adulthood. I too, sent him out into life believing he should be ready to make his own choices at eighteen, too stupid to realize I'd left him just as unprepared for adulting, if not more than I'd been.

Times evolve, the world gets bigger, and we have more access to information. His childhood was the opposite of the sheltered one I'd had. But I've since come to understand how much more confusing all of that can make things. And when children don't feel comfortable enough to talk to their parents they are often left with a lot of confusion and repressed emotions. I, like my parents before me talked at William without really talking with him as he grew up.

Subconsciously, I overcompensated for my own crappy upbringing as parents usually do. I vowed that my son would feel loved. I hugged him and told him frequently how much I loved and missed him when he went back to his dad's. I didn't know he was doing all he could to please both of us because we were each sad to see him leave. I didn't know he'd taken all of that on. His father and I had separated at such a young age for him I had no idea how much living in two separate homes affected my boy, because we didn't talk about it.

We didn't talk about how he felt, but we sure did talk a lot about how I felt. I leaned on him too much, shared too much and expected that he'd understand things he had no way of grasping in his young life.

 It's so freaking weird how often parents expect children to know things they've not been taught (just as it had happened with me) and how much we all assume is just innate which is not. We can forget what it's like to be a kid far too quickly. We forget how very vulnerable children are at any given moment when it comes to their emotional lives. We mistakenly feel that if we are keeping them safe in the ways we believe they need that's all there is too it, without considering how they feel at various ages.

I really wanted William to have fun in life, all the fun I hadn't been allowed. Toys had been so lacking for me I couldn't stop filling his room with them. With clothing to bedding to birthday cakes we celebrated cartoon characters, superheroes, sports, and anything he showed an interest in. Throughout the winter months we'd spend hours on the phone planning the next great summer adventures and Southern California had plenty to choose from. Between beaches, bays, parks, camping, zoos, and an assortment of amusement parks we filled our days with excitement. William rolled through the summers skateboarding or rollerblading everywhere, spending days at the beach on one sort of board or another and he seemed happy.

What sucks about compensation and making up for our own stuff is it's an easy way to miss what your own child really needs. They don't need a bunch more of the stuff we never got. They may not even need, like or want any of those things.

Like those who came before me I did the best I could with the tools I had at the time but that doesn't mean what I did wasn't absolute shit for my child. I just wouldn't be able to see that for years to come. We think if they had what we missed out on that's all they need to be happy and fulfilled. Just as we think if another adult has things we want they should be happy.

We think as adults we automatically know what's best for small children. It is hard as hell to hear you fucked up just as badly if not worse than the last generation. It can take a long time to come to grips with that, especially when you are unraveling your own shit along the way. And this is exactly what my life would become filled with as time went on. Many times, I would not be able to hear what my son had to say, which I think had a lot to do with him being unwilling to hear what I had to say later on.

So, in the spirit of summers past I reached out to my son to see if we could arrange for a visit. I thought we'd plan a vacation, so I scouted out a great rental overlooking Puget Sound. He suggested the quaint little hamlet of Gig Harbor, Washington, which proved to be as auspicious as it sounded. The town and the cottage we found were gorgeous and included a family of deer that ambled through the front lawn for daily visits. But the boy who'd seemed so happy of summers past was not who came on this vacation.

I was so oblivious. I showed up with what I thought was a special gift, along with a heartfelt letter which I presented with pride, thinking I could still guide my son, not realizing perhaps I never had. This week turned out to be the beginning of the emotional roller coaster that would become the new normal in my life for quite a while. We did our best, we took in a movie at a theater that offered cocktails, played some board games, and cooked a thanksgiving-style meal. We spent a full week together, which in the end showed me how far apart we had become.

I thought I was the parent, and things would happen to me first so I could share my experiences with him as a means of supporting his growth. I couldn't know that some of these realizations had happened for William much earlier, because of the glaring gap between us. He hadn't told me that I was an integral part in his deepening unhappiness.

All too soon I'd come to understand that the lack of compassion I had for myself was even more lacking when it came to my son. My parents had instilled a hatred for excess weight in me that would spew all over him as I unleashed my own pent-up fears and frustrations. Like lava erupting from a volcano, a rage would arise unexpectedly, and I was too blind in my lack of empathy at the time to see the layers of pain building upon his body.

CHAPTER 11: COMING TO TERMS

Doing your best as parents can still be an epic fail.

The safety nets we weave for ourselves out of the fabric of our childhood fail the test far more often than we can even imagine. This leaves us spinning in lives we probably didn't choose, seeking safety in our work and comfort in our food. We distract ourselves with shopping and entertainment, believing we are fine but knowing from deep within we are not. And, of course, ignoring anything that hints that we are not in a good place. We ascribe to avoidant coping behaviors and adapt as if that is normal and healthy. We look for the answers externally because we were so often encouraged to ignore ourselves inwardly.

Many of us just learned to believe we were fine because we were told that so often. Screaming babies are told not to cry and that they are fine. Confused children are told to be quite, often sent to our rooms without explanation. As parents we can devalue our children's early feelings of crisis because we assume they will pass. We learn to think of behavior as a phase. Ignoring a child's feelings can lead to serious repressed pain. Telling a child things will pass is not nearly as helpful for the child as teaching them to understand what they feel and how to process and release it. I thought William was fine. Even when I finally had to admit I was dyslexic I still thought I was fine. But with a little digging I learned that drinking during pregnancy causes dyslexia, thanks mom.

Photo of mom smoking and drinking before I was born.

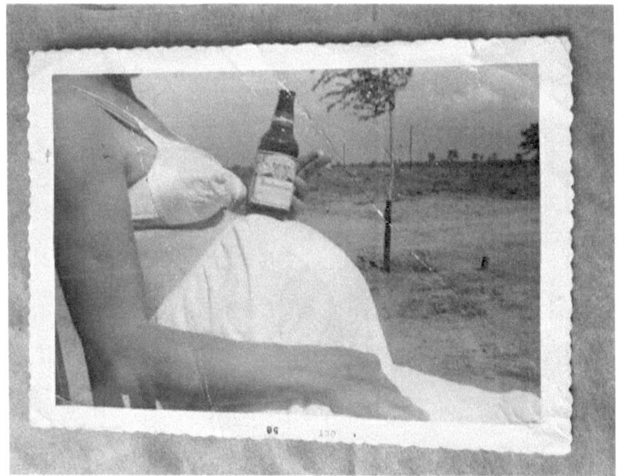

The visit with William had left me in a deep state of panic. Of course, because I'd not given it any thought, I expected that my son would just fall out of childhood, into his life like I had. The difference was I disliked both of my parents and my son did not. I was motivated because I didn't want to have to ask them for anything. I think my son was crushed because he had tried so hard to be what we all wanted, and I paid more attention to things that didn't matter at all.

It would be a long time before I'd be able to look back at my actions and accept the blame for the resentment I had caused him. I didn't understand the ways William needed me because I had not been allowed to need my parents in many ways at all.

The only expectation I had was that his life would turn out better than my own. When their lives don't follow the picture in our minds as parents we are left lost, frustrated, and filled with doubt and fear. It breaks open our hearts, digs into our souls and for me, sent me into an even deeper dive of research.

William had admittedly become stuck and out of balance which cut me to my core. But until I took care of my own stuff I wouldn't be able to understand his. So, like the burn felt after a day in the sun, my eyes gradually opened to my failures. Bit by bit they finally broke me and tore my heart to shreds.

I would be brought to my knees in regret and agony. Our hearts, emotions, and compassion become entwined in everything our child ever does during their lives. They often have no clue of the impact they have on us, certainly less if they have no kids of their own. In the meantime, I plowed ahead in oblivious mom mode and planned another trip to see my son, this one for a whole month's time.

Consciousness has various levels and self-awareness can be somewhat on a spectrum once you open the door. But the alternative, the one where we hide away behind denial and live only on the surface is where we can do the most damage to ourselves and others. That's what I had done most of my life and that was what made it so easy to believe I was right, to think I knew what was best, and not just for myself but for everyone else. That's all bullshit. But when you are in it, when you are acting like an authoritarian, your mind fully believes you know, and you are certain you are the most correct person on the planet.

Fortunately, I was (slowly) becoming aware of the danger in that narrow vision and close-minded perspective. I was getting ready to leave that false persona imprinted in childhood, release all the emotional baggage I'd drug around and move into my real self...eventually. And my son was a big part of those shifts.

For my stay near my boy, I had booked a place but at the last minute decided to cancel. I had no idea why. The next one I found happened to be about two blocks from Keith's house. I was using a site that didn't show addresses until you booked so I had no way of knowing this. I took it as a good sign. I'd been talking with Keith about our son, and he was open to doing all we could to help turn things around for him.

This longer stay was no better than the first. William's dad and I went to see a professional who suggested anxiety. William's weight had me worried constantly about his health. When he said he was not feeling well one day, I panicked. I insisted that this had to be the bottom line and we all needed to find a way for his health to become a priority. Later it was clear that both Keith and William thought I was overreacting, and I would later learn they'd both decided I was the root of all problem years beforehand.

Somewhere along the way (it seems to me) William had tried to shrink into the background of life, maybe because he had felt so unsafe emotionally around me. In a way he's mastered the art of looking content, so it looks like there is nothing to worry about.

I'd gone on this second trip in hope of reestablishing our bond and opening lines of communication, not to stumble upon a tragic realization, but I had to face facts. I had let my son down tremendously and how all that was tied to my own past was coming to the surface.

I remembered when his father had returned from Australia and came down on me because I hadn't been teaching William as much as he felt I should have. It wasn't like I'd been taught anything myself before going to school. There were zero resources at hand to help me sort through this. Keith had spent plenty of time around my parents and had witnessed the neglect and emotional abuse I'd suffered. But neither of us knew how much those things had shut me down emotionally and compromised my ability to empathize.

Much like my own son I had learned to carry myself in a way that projected confidence, when in my case was in actuality just indifference. I remember buying my son so many toys and books, usually trying to find educational ones. From my limited perspective I was doing right by my boy. Keith did not feel the same way or hesitate to share his disappointment with me. That's me, NOT meeting expectations since the late 50's.

Returning home, I became totally immersed in research.

CHAPTER 12: FINDING "SOULITUDE"

The value in life is not found in what one owns, rather in who one learns themselves to truly be.

That trip left me restless in ways that research and the gym didn't cure. I was back to eyeing my house now. That place was an oddity. Everyone who visited seemed to just love it and I didn't see why. I liked it well enough, but it hadn't felt at home like the last one I had.

Derek and I had bought our first home ever together when we were both in our thirties. We invested three years of our time in renovation, ripping out a ceiling in one bath that looked like the top of a meringue pie, and dredging a four-foot trench in the floor to fix some flooding under the slab. We spackled, painted, tiled, built a new closet, a patio cover, traded out the old windows for new and installed a French door. We dug out the creepy cacti, one almost breaking my foot in the process. We planted a lawn, a garden, roses, palms, and fruit trees. And we had a pool. We loved it there...until we didn't. Or at least until I didn't.

Buying a first home is both exciting and panic inducing. We had a terrible realtor who kept dragging us to places out of our price range. But the powers that be stepped in and as I was driving one day I saw it, exactly where I wanted to be. I passed a lush green canyon that was very centrally located and that's where we landed! My first manifestation! The drawback was the neighborhood's severe lack of curb appeal once you got past that lush canyon. The whole time we lived there I longed for a greener space. The next one, the I was now pacing around in, was greener.

It was situated in an established neighborhood adorned by hundreds of majestically tall trees. Their shadows cast a serene presence of natural beauty. They served as a bit of a hiding place for a community with a hometown feel.

One of my reasons for not liking that house had to do with the man who I refer to as my ex from hell. He was the first one to spend time with me there, which was really nothing more than adding a very painful finale to a twenty-year dance with a narcissist. But he also brought the lesson of authoritarian behavior by repeating the words "things don't always have to be the way you think they should be". He was right about that.

This house was also the place where I learned how to be alone for the first time. It would be where I'd finally fall back enough to see my long series of serious relationships had been my attempt at making up for the lack of love as a kid. The last was with Gerard, who I dated for close to three years. The plus side is we have had a great friendship for nearly fifteen years now. The hard part, our breakup threw me into a downward spiral like none before. Maybe because I was in my fifties, I don't know. I also didn't know this was my line in the sand when it came to what love and relationships mean. Maybe my higher self knew because it took a lot of soul-searching to make peace with being on my own.

At that time, *alone* still meant loneliness. At first, I stopped caring. I barely moved. At work my coworkers would ask if I needed anything as if I was incapable of getting up from behind my desk. All of life felt like drudgery and even my son told me he needed a break from me. I looked at my reflection realizing I was the best I had left, feeling certain I was not much at all. Who was I on my own?

In thirty-five years, I'd not spent more than three or four months alone. Did I just feel so unloved I wanted to prove I was loveable? But two husbands, two fiancées, two live-ins, and countless dates later that hadn't changed. I'd had to face that pain I'd brought to some of these men. But during it all I felt entitled to find something deeper with someone, even though it was my own emotional shutdown that was blocking me all along.

Gerard was also the one who opened my eyes to deeper connections in an unexpected way. On a road trip to Vegas, we'd stopped by my dad's gravesite. We stood there in the middle of nowhere next to that burial plot and I felt nothing. I think the pain this man had caused me with his dismissive criticism and neglect had numbed me. I hadn't even been aware that my father's birthday was one day after Gerards - until he pointed it out.

Love had been illusive for me since I'd arrived on the planet, but it wouldn't be much longer until it would knock me silly. But first I had to be ok on my own. It was grueling. I would go and sit in my closet to cry at times because the fits of pain came in such sweeping waves. didn't want my neighbors to hear. But I was learning how to deal with it. This "soulitude", a silence for my soul turned out to be just what I needed. First came the weekends. If no one invited me out, I was determined not to seek any company. Then there was the Superbowl, no parties for me. Then a heart-wrenching Valentine's Day.

Slowly, I became stronger. Finally, several grueling months passed, and my perspective changed. A day can be labeled any type of holiday but spending it alone doesn't label you as defective. When the number one thing we seek is safety, knowing you are safe by yourself in critical. What we don't stop to think about is how much of the time we are truly safe. Measure it in moments and we see it's quite often. It's only insecurities and hidden fears telling us otherwise.

I still stood in that house with growing distaste. The more I was being moved out of the familiar the more open-minded and accepting I was becoming. Things did not, in fact, have to be the way I thought they should be.

My identity was not to be found in accomplishments or by the company I kept, it was in there all along just waiting for me to open the door.

CHAPTER 13: WHEN A SPIRITUAL DOOR OPENS, VISIT THE HOLY LAND

Spirituality doesn't have to box you into the conditions of religion beliefs.

Maybe because spirituality shouldn't have been the last thing that was on my mind, I was invited to join in on a trip to Israel. It may have been a little indicator of the spiritual things to come.

There I was, no income, no relationship, no direction - getting the opportunity to take the trip of a lifetime. It was a leap of faith for sure given my finances at the time. But it was also one of the earliest signs of how I was being provided for without exception.

Now and again, Gerard will decide it's time to take a trip

and I'm grateful and happy to be included. All the travel I've done outside of trips with William or visiting people have been motivated by someone else. After all, as a kid I'd learned to believe what I wanted had no meaning.

The Middle East was packed with the history Gerard enjoys and was absolutely intriguing to me regardless of the ongoing tension. So, in July of 2013 off to the Promised Land we went.

I landed in Tel Aviv to find my luggage still in Paris where we'd changed planes. Gerard and I had taken separate flights. So, I was grateful when the lovely member of the Israeli Army I'd been speaking with since Paris offered help with the missing bags.

Normally I wouldn't have cared but the twenty-four hours I'd just traveled had taken its toll on my attire. And I knew we were booked for an early morning tour. I was panicked but in the end all I could do was wait for the baggage to be delivered to the hotel, which to my surprise was right on the banks of the sea. As we strolled over to the water I grabbed both a toothbrush and a coconut ice cream cone and felt a bit better. But not as overjoyed as when my luggage arrived later that evening.

Israel is a hauntingly beautiful place to visit.

No matter a person's beliefs or viewpoints this area has so much historical meaning you don't have to believe anything in particular to feel the presence of the energy there. Being present in these lands brought a change to my perspective as well as my own energy. In Jerusalem, considered the holiest place in the world, we could physically feel the magnitude of the Church of the Holy Sepulcher as we entered. I nearly passed out from the heat but still managed to reach the Wailing (or Western) wall and place a note within the stones. And then we solemnly walked the trail of the Via Dolorosa where Jesus is said to have carried his cross, now curiously lined with shops and vendors.

We spent a day in Nazareth touring St. Joseph's church and Joseph's workshop, ambling along where Jesus was said to have lived part of his life. I dipped my feet in the Jordan River, we were driven past the Sea of Galilee, spent a day of discovery in the mountains of Masada, floated in the Dead Sea, took in a local flea market, and took a winding cab ride along a cobblestone street to their most renowned restaurant, the Old Man in the Sea. Everywhere we went the food was the freshest either of us could remember having. One day, Gerard took a tour that sounded a bit too historic for me, so I walked up the coast for a visit to the oldest port in the world and had lunch by myself overlooking the Mediterranean Sea.

The people were lovely and amazingly friendly, in fact remarkably so for me in particular. Nearly every day, sometimes more than once, a local resident would approach me speaking Hebrew. Sometimes they would go as far as crossing the street to talk to me. At times Gerard would be next to me, other times his attention would be elsewhere. Every single time the person would be shocked to hear me speak English and their demeanor changed entirely once they worked out the fact that I didn't understand them at all. By the end of our eight-day stay it had become quite eerie and left me feeling like I'd just missed out on an important message, their energy had been so strong. To this day, I still have no idea and now I wish I'd asked one of them to accompany me to find translation.

Our last day in Tel Aviv was the Sabbath, so most things were closed. It was a day of rest, which we needed as our most stressful adventure happened the day prior in Bethlehem. We'd taken a tour to this sacred town situated in the Palestinian territory. As we approached an exceptionally large brick and barbed wire structure (that looked quite prison-esque) our tour guide had to leave us. That was not in the brochure. Walking forward hesitantly, we each looked back over our shoulders, but the guide instructed us to keep going. We were to cross through a set of gates as it was there we'd find our Palestinian guide waiting. He failed to mention the dozen or so heavily armed guards we were to encounter along the way. This was a definite test of my faith.

Once across, having met our guide, we made our way

to what is believed to be the birthplace of Jesus. Throngs of people descended down narrow flight of stairs, pushing their way together toward the entrance, with no space between bodies. My breath stopped. It was too great of a personal experience to miss out on because of claustrophobia but I stood still.

I looked around at the high ceilings inhaling deeply. Our guide gently took my arm and asked that I follow him. I found myself at the exit. We were entering backwards, bypassing the crowds entirely. There I stood, staring to the floor, at a well-worn placard in the shape of star surrounded by marble. People were on their knees, bent over in prayer, touching this holy ground. I fought my instincts, knowing others were waiting but taking the time I needed to revel in the peace I felt here, a moment to be remembered for eternity.

I know we all learn to see things from the perspective of our own experiences and beliefs. Beliefs which are formed from not only those experiences but conditioning as well. But outside of all that we are allowed to feel energy. We can either choose to open our minds to it or not. There is more to life that what we believe or see. This trip was just the beginning for me.

The guide and I sat on a ledge waiting on the rest of the tour to make their way through and he started asking me personal questions, enough that I was relieved to see

Gerard. When the day of sightseeing and shopping were complete, we began the harrowing trek back across the border. As the line snaked its way toward the huge iron turn stalls, we were separated. One of the men nearby was leering at me, I thought he might be going to spit in my direction. He growled that I was responsible for their apartheid. Wow. Gerard, on the other hand, was having a nice conversation but later explained the man's comments to me.

So, we spent our last day in Israel reflecting on what we'd experienced and then as Gerard headed home, I set off for a four-day adventure by myself in Paris. Since it was a layover anyway, I decided to layover a bit longer. I'd had enough experiences in working with the French to know it wasn't a trip I would take otherwise and breakfast the next morning reminded me why.

I was just well versed enough in their language to know the woman at the desk speaking to her work mate was calling me a "fat pig" as I looked over the complimentary breakfast choices of bread and more bread. By the time I made my way to her counter she'd affixed her professional smile and offered a greeting. The renegade in me knew what to do. I smiled right back and then told her I understood enough French to know exactly what she had just said. There is nothing like catching a snooty French woman off guard, it brought out such a nice shade of red. For the remainder of the stay, she appeared to be gracious and tried her best to be helpful, but I didn't need her. I had made friends with the wonderful non-French man who owned the market across the street. He kindly and pleasantly helped me negotiate the metro and offered other helpful suggestions for my stay.

The Parisians alternated between fun and obnoxious, which mirrored my relationships with my French friends back home; fortunately, my friends leaned more toward fun. Paris is grand and exuberant. The powerful looming sight of the Eiffel Tower up close, a tranquil river taxi ride on the Seine. I lit a candle for my son in the Cathedral of Notre Dame and walked past the vivacious exterior of the Moulin Rouge. I strolled from the Arc de Triomphe through Champs-Élysées to the Louvre where the line was too long. So, I instead toured the remarkable Musée d'Orsay. I went up the hill to Montmartre and bought some art to bring back; my best purchase because the cheese I'd bought left my luggage smelling like a farm. Neither the cheese nor the luggage survived.

CHAPTER 14:
THE STUFFING
OF AVOCADOS

Only within the open mind of inquiry do we honestly find the root of our dysfunction.

The grandeur of Paris and the Holiness of Israel had made my life's concerns seem temporarily insignificant, and I was at greater peace. But coming home nothing had changed. The scale still showed me that I was a fat person and the bank let me know I was still unemployed. The house still echoed in loneliness.

It was my brilliant William who suggested that I try hypnotherapy.

My son, as it turned out, was far better at giving advice at this point in our lives than I had possibly ever been. William is unbelievably sweet, kind, caring, thoughtful and really an incredible human being. A gentle soul who deserved much better than what I could muster when I became his mother; and I certainly didn't deserve this amazing child to be delivered into my dysfunctional world. But it was his recognition of that very dysfunction that prompted him to seek more understanding about what had happened in his life. Awareness had knocked on his door long before ever approaching mine.

He thought if hypnotherapy had helped his dad quit smoking it could be worth a shot for me too. At this point, what did I really have to lose? Something like this normally took me weeks to investigate. But this time I didn't overthink things. With just a few clicks of the mouse I had made an appointment to give it a trial run. I'd envisioned somewhat of a reprogramming of my brain to get myself on track. I mean, hypnosis was the stuff that could make you quack like a duck, right?

So, I took that mindset off to my very first appointment and it was there I met Sean, my new hypnotherapist. He looked so much like my half-brother Barry it was crazy. I sat in his office; a bit mesmerized as he explained the process while simultaneously trying to remember that he was not related to me.

Barry, my half-brother had been absent from my life since 1990, which uniquely coincided with the time of my father's death and subsequent hospitalization of our mother two weeks later. How my half-brother chose to handle everything our family was facing at that time was, for me at least, beyond shocking.

What were the odds that I'd find someone who looked so similar to do this work with? But when it came to synchronicities this was only the smallest of drops in what would become an exceptionally large bucket. Maybe Sean's appearance was a warning of the unpleasant family dynamics that would be at the forefront of our work together.

As we talked about the elephant in the room (my own enormous weight, of course), Sean wanted to know if I'd be comfortable talking more about my life. It caught me off guard. I must have still been picturing the hypnosis you see on a stage and been waiting for the watch to start dangling in front of my eyes.

After a good half hour of what was more like chatting with a friend, Sean asked if I wanted to give hypnosis a try and began to guide me into relaxation. It was quite peaceful, really. I envisioned myself on a somewhat mystical version of a beach at night. The dark sky atop the crashing black and white waves was very soothing. He then asked me to begin descending a staircase and to relax more with each step, delving deeper into the realm of my subconscious. And then I was to find myself in front of a door, which I was to describe to Sean in detail. In front of me stood a beautiful glossy white door with an arched frame which Sean asked me to open. He then asked if I could continue inside and walk a little further.

I began to speak in the voice of a small child. As if I had been transported back in time, I found myself smack dab in the house in which I'd grown up. I could see it all so vividly. It was, no joke, like I was there in real time. The long forgotten and somewhat blurry mural sized photo of Bryce Canyon in all its orange glory covering most of one wall. The gold-covered chairs and the multicolor tablecloth. And there was my mother coming in from the kitchen to set a small plate of food in front of me.

In the distance was Sean's voice, anchoring me in real time, wondering what I was doing. I described my surroundings and the stuffed avocado my mother had proudly presented as my meal. Sean mentioned what an interesting lunch that was for such a little girl. And the adult in me knew it too. My mom had been one of those women, an early supporter, before the women's movement had even begun, who took on jobs that had been meant only for men back in the day. She fancied herself a chef.

As I sat there my mother appeared with a second serving and Sean again asked what I was doing. I could feel shame rush to the surface, my face becoming hot as he asked if I'd wanted that second portion. As my childlike voice, smaller now and quivering, whispered a simple no, a flood of tears was unleashed and began streaming down my face, splattering onto my hands. Sean had asked why I agreed to seconds and I managed to whimper, "Because the little girl will disappear!" and I felt lost to the weight of my own sorrow.

Crying in those moments was like nothing I'd experienced before. The release of a pain that has been so deeply hidden, a pain that had frozen the little girl in me back in that time, was nothing short of magnificent. It seemed as if I could be there as my adult self, present to assist my child self and just hold the space needed to release all of that hidden and repressed sadness. I felt like I'd witnessed my own miracle.

I came back to full consciousness, shocked by the encounter I'd had with my past. The irony of the avocados being stuffed were indicative of how I'd learned to stuff myself as a child in order to be seen, to be noticed, to feel alive, anything instead of existing in the usual state of silence.

I had revisited one of the earliest moments when my body had learned to take on the burden of my emotions. It was too soon for me to recognize this as neglect, or to understand why I was using food to get attention. Or even know why I had been so desperate for that attention, but it was a start. A big start.

Sean and I talked for a moment about my mom. I described the picture she had painted of herself for me over the years, one who proudly displayed the scars she bore on her chest as she described her time as a welder during World War II. Somewhere, there must have been an amazing woman inside the person I had tried so hard to please during that meal, yet what I remembered most was the unkindness of a woman who was very mean. My mom seemed to be unhappy most of the time. If she wasn't upset with me, she was upset with my dad, which would have been a great opening for us to forge a bond, dad, and I, had he taken any interest in such a thing. But, as much as I disliked how she was, I unwittingly became a lot like her when it came to interacting with my own child. And it was not too hard to understand why unhappiness seemed normal in my life, I'd learned it to be normal from my own mother.

Nonetheless, on this day, here in this tiny office, the first of many miracles had happened. I was left feeling freer than I had at any time before. The release had been so powerful. Deeply hidden emotion and anxiety had finally loosened their holds from the repressed nooks and crannies of my subconscious, leading me to believe I was in peace, fully aware and healed. For that moment, I truly was.

CHAPTER 15: RESPECT THE PROCESS

The question becomes: why don't we invest our free time toward feeling better, rather than continuously distracting ourselves from feeling so poorly...

It was hard to tell when or how that feeling of being on top of the world faded, but soon I was back at the grocery store in the isle of my greatest demise. As I stood in front of the ice cream selections I started questioning if not all things needed to happen as quickly as I'd led myself to believe. That's the thing about beliefs, there's nothing fact-based about them. They really are just how we hope things will go.

I'd bumped up against one more hidden memory. It accounted for precisely one of the many bars that were conspiring to cage me within my food prison. The way out of that special little cell was going to take time. It was easy to forget that getting there hadn't happened quickly. One visit hadn't opened all of the flood gates, even though it seemed to at the time. There was nothing to be done except to keep doing the work. So, I booked a second appointment and went to the gym to contemplate what I'd actually gotten myself into. And what I was going to do about my future.

My attempt at Airbnb hosting wasn't the greatest but at least helped me decide against getting roommates. I talked to a few contractors about building a small granny flat in the backyard but found it would exhaust the majority of the limited reserves I had. So, I turned back to my buddies: garage sale and Offer Up, who were fortunately willing to lend a hand.

Clothes and smaller pieces of furniture all went flying off the blankets thrown over the driveway starting around 6:00 a.m. Because that's when the kind folks from across the border like to shop to get the best inventory. Being so close to Mexico was a blessing in this way and after a sale or two it became easy to distinguish the true professionals from the novice Saturday shopper. The lone stragglers who spoke the most broken English would haggle for pennies in pricing; where the real deal buyers would arrive in groups of two and three, scope out the place in minutes, and make one big pile in the center. They would wait patiently as you went through adding up your intended pricing and pay without a second glance. After five hours of this as the clock neared 11:00 a.m. a few trucks would roll through hoping to score everything for free.

I was blessed to live in a great cul-de-sac where many of the residents had been homeowners since the development was built in 1971! Not one of them said a word about the constant flow of traffic for those sales. At times they'd stop by and pick up something of interest and visit a bit.

This was one of the few times my weight had played in my favor. The shopping I did was focused on home goods rather than clothing and as a result I had a lot of cool, saleable shit. And that's the reason I found a new friend, who will always be known as my Craigslist friend. Who, in fact, is having a garage sale herself at the exact moment I'm typing this! I had posted the cutest Pier One Christmas pillows for sale and on New Year's Eve, enter Nita! Here we are, years down the road, friends, confidants, not only my ride or die but also my other partner in crime for the writing of this book.

When a kindred soul enters your space, you sense something different, which is exactly what happened on the day we met. As she parked in front of the house, I grabbed the pillows and walked out to be greeted with a huge smile, like that of an old friend. She couldn't contain her joy in finding those pillows because she'd been searching for them for her granddaughter for a while. We were so comfortable with each other I invited her in the house. Two short hours and several sales later we walked back to her car having exchanged numbers.

I couldn't wait to chat more, so I invited her over for a glass *(or several)* of wine and she was instantly intrigued by the random emptiness of my home. She was right, it did look like things had been removed haphazardly, because they had. I admitted to my new friend that I had no idea what I was doing.

In the back of my mind, I'd been kicking around the idea that I would have to move but it was now feeling a whole lot more like I wanted to move. That house, like so many other things in my life, was nothing special to me. It was just one more of those things that looked good from the outside but truthfully was just disappointing. That's how Nita (not fully certain yet if I was insane) became not only my regular customer but my garage sale partner and future travel buddy. When I say we've had some unbelievable times together, that is no exaggeration.

The time had come for my second visit with Sean. Strolling into the building through the breezeway of a surprisingly open concept design from what I believed was the seventies, I contemplated taking the stairs. The elevator appeared to have been transported from Europe in the 1920s and during my last visit had made the ghastly snorting and spurting sounds you might expect from what must have been a once great beast. I wonder now if that had been somewhat a symbol, a silent notation of a deeply hidden fear of returning to the past. Hypnotherapy would become that for me, a constant return to my illustrious childhood.

Of course, how often do we really take the time to stop in life and seriously look back at what happened to us as kids? As I'm writing this, childhood trauma is becoming a hot topic but when I first began this intensive deep dive that was not the case. Even now, there are many who still avoid this topic like the plague, and perhaps denial is just that – a plague. And honestly had I not been shoved down this path, I'd probably still be just where I was.

It's too easy to think of trauma as just the bad shit. The stuff movies are made of; divorce, death, destruction, abuse, that really scary stuff. My experiences had included none of those and it is even kind of a stretch to think of a chubby little girl as being neglected. My parents weren't horrible people but that didn't mean my childhood wasn't horrific. What they were missing was awareness. Neither of them were emotionally self-aware or at all concerned about what I needed, and without emotional connection there is no bonding. Parental emotional self-awareness is vital to successful parenting.

Life often becomes a series of expectations that kind of all flow together. We come in free of it all, smiles become laughs, crawling turns into unsteady steps, as we are curiously ready to become our own heart's desires. All along the way we pick up a bag and fill it with the fears, expectations, and missed opportunities our parents have projected upon us. New shapes and sizes are cast into the bag as we enter society and learn of those conditions and expectations; any unresolved pain or confusion falling heavily to the bottom. When it's time we pick up that bag and then off we go, rarely looking back, even rarer looking inward, forgetting all about our heart's desire. Just dragging all of that bullshit around. We keep trying to look as happy as possible because that was the type of emotion that was acceptable as we grew up.

Until the time we are called to unravel it all, and here I was in Sean's office to do just that. I had such distaste for my mom I thought the bag that I carried was filled with her crap. She paid so little attention to me I'd once put a paper grocery bag over my head and walked straight into a Joshua tree. There I stood, stuck to the tree, and screaming at the top of my little lungs with blood gushing onto the dry desert ground.

What I remember most of that day is the number of times my mom told the story about how I had almost poked my eye out. Like I was of a responsible enough age to let wander around freely among the cacti, carrying a brown paper grocery bag. The thorny blade had punctured through one side of my nose exiting the other but somehow hadn't warranted a visit to the doctor. I strongly believe that was the reason I later needed surgery to correct a deviated septum.

At Sean's direction, I'd again wound my way down the staircase of relaxation and had arrived in a situation with a different brown grocery bag, but this time Mom wasn't the central character. Now it was my dad's beaming face that greeted me as he set a bag filled with day-old pastries on the counter. His contribution to our happiness were these gross fruit-filled pies, glistening with a hard sugar glazed outer crust, which unfortunately accounted for the majority of the bag's contents.

Each night, the moments after dinner transformed into a magical encounter as he'd been waiting in anticipation for his dessert. I secretly despised the stale contents of that bag but pretended to be swept into the magic just to be part of his happiness, any happiness. Those were the rare and brief seconds when we shared one small thing. Again, I'd given away a bit of my own agency to eat something I didn't want just to feel a moment of connection. A theme was beginning to show its ugly self repeatedly. Had it not been for hypnotherapy that ugliness would have remained hidden, and I wouldn't have released that pain.

When food, or anything really, holds such a place of supreme importance to parents during those early years it can set up a child for failure in some insidious ways. Holding food in reverence as both my parents did played a large part in the construction of my food prison. Each unintended slight thereafter added another bar until the door had firmly clanged shut leaving my emotional body hidden behind and food left to stand guard in place of healthy coping.

As Sean and I moved forward I again found peace by releasing that old, stale, trapped pain through tears. Tears that were not painful in those moments but instead a beautiful clean release. It was a way to honor the child inside who'd been suffering for years and had not been equipped to deal with the experiences at the time.

Going back through the lens of an adult's logic is an amazing tool. Wafting there deep in my subconscious I could attribute my dad's penchant for sweets as his way of compensating for the lack in his own childhood and find a bit of forgiveness. Removing the pain and reframing events in hypnotherapy had released those specific moments hold on me. I'm certain my dad didn't understand that those sweets he considered a real treat were instead treating me to a food addiction. At least I was taking steps now to eradicate it.

CHAPTER 16: THE UNRAVELING

All personality traits are not innate but instead molded by childhood experiences.

There I sat trembling at a gas station on my way for another visit with Sean. There was plenty of time to spare, the tank was already full, but I was rushing around like there was a fire. I was excited for this next visit, in fact the opposite of anxious. So, I forced myself to stay right there and take a deep breath and just wait. I craned my neck for a look around at the other pumps, which all sat empty. As I gave it more time it was easy to recognize this was a familiar feeling. I rushed around a lot. My mom used to ask me why I was in such a hurry. This was the beauty of increasing my own personal awareness. Things exactly like this. Things we think we just have to live with, things that had been going on my whole life without my caring. I cared now.

At the appointment I cozied into the usual chair in Sean's office, threw my feet up on the ottoman and told him the tale of the gas station. He said he believed it was innate and just a personality trait, but I wasn't having it. I knew he was the professional I was paying to help sort this stuff out, but because of the circumstances I was certain this was something deeper.

Back into the depth of my subconscious we went and that day I was to relive another conversation with my mom, except this one had nothing to do with moving too fast. In the darkness of the room my family had referred to as the *back room* stood my mother, ensconced in a cloud of steam rising from the clothes she was ironing. A dampened pile at her side, waiting their turn.

I wonder if she might have taken in ironing as a source of income because who was wearing all of these freshly pressed garments? My mom stayed at home and Dad was a mechanic. We didn't go to church. My parents had built that house on their own after homesteading the land. I still have a photo of an outhouse they used before adding a bathroom.

The house stood at the end of a rutty and rocky dirt road. My dad did something called "dragging" the road where he'd chain a giant railroad tie behind his truck and drive up and down the road to smooth it. The running water in the house came from him "hauling water" in, which was then transferred to a big tank outside. Taking out the trash meant walking a quarter of a mile into the desert while watching out for scorpions and rattlesnakes and tossing garbage down a ravine onto someone else's land. We were our own little third-world country.

I watched as my mother used a spray bottle to mist the already damp piece she was ready to press. I was probably eight at that time and I had a point to be there, I wanted her help understanding something I'd been hearing about at school. A lot of the kids had been talking about their parents wedding anniversaries like it was a very special celebration, which my parents had never mentioned. I wanted to know more. My mother slowly straightened from her ironing-board hunch. She turned her eyes to me and said, "Well, if you must know", huffily proceeding to tell me how she and Dad had gotten married after I was born. She looked like the weight of the world had just crushed her and she was mad as hell.

At that age I didn't know what any of that meant. She glared at me like it was my fault. "I'm sorry," I whimpered, hoping to calm whatever seas raged within her. "Stop saying you're sorry. You never mean it!" she screamed at me. With nothing left to do but get out of the way, I left the room before any tears fell. The adult watching this unfold knew my mom had projected a big heaping pile of guilt and shame right onto my small frame in those moments. She had left me without explanation in a cloud of confusion and pain.

What happened as I sat behind the wheel at that gas station were part of a false belief system I'd created about myself during those exact type of traumatic childhood experiences. The belief that I was the problem, I was in the way or just plain wrong for being there at all meant that I needed to move fast to avoid as much blame or shame as I could. It manifested as a low-level anxiety which caused me to worry about my presence everywhere I went. This meeting with Sean led me to the core of it and began the healing process I needed to release that belief system. I don't recall even one time when my mother talked about emotions with anyone so I'm sure she never let go of that shame herself.

Emotions happen all day long, every single day and depending on our experiences they will affect us each differently. Without proper guidance as children and without being given the tools needed to navigate ourselves emotionally, we become very vulnerable and susceptible to increasing levels of anxiety because we are effected by everything around us. We lack the basic foundation needed to successfully navigate life in a balanced, happy, and peaceful manner. These hidden moments live in our subconscious, thus blocking us from conscious behavior.

As parents I believe we all make a lot of assumptions about our kids because we have not taken the time to reflect deeply enough on the vulnerability of our own childhood. Our subconscious has chosen to hide all of the feelings because we don't know what to do with them. We just want them to go away. We just want it to stop. But in order to overcome this, we must become emotionally self-aware adults ourselves and have real honest conversations with our kids. All of our insecurities are rooted in moments just like this.

Neither of my parents were very tuned into any of this. Toward the end of the fifties, Mom was proudly cooking in a tiny American diner in Long Beach, CA. when she met my dad who was a customer at the counter. She was forty-one at the time, married, and raising my ten-year-old half-brother, Barry. Regardless, they began an affair which resulted in me. She then turned her back on Barry and his dad to eventually make my fifty-three-year-old father her fourth husband. Apparently after I was born.

The shame I'd unwittingly unleashed that day talking with my mom made no sense to me then, and to be honest, it still doesn't. It was outdated. But here's what I can say, as a kid, that day made me feel like I was the embodiment of that shame. It's impossible to have your mother's rage directed toward you and not feel like you're the problem. My son would later help me see how I'd done the same to him in some of the exact same ways. Harsh words left unexplained are daggers thrown straight into the psyche of a child.

In those moments with Sean though, releasing that and handing it back to my mom within the confines of my subconscious was self-actualizing gold. Sometimes we carry burdens that have been projected onto us from pure ignorance; but it's not every day we get to relinquish them to their rightful owners. More and more I found myself in gratitude. More and more I was simply finding myself. Unpacking emotional baggage is like unloading what burdens your soul.

CHAPTER 17: A GLIMPSE OF A MORE PEACEFUL SELF

How is it possible to get in touch with yourself if you don't pay attention to how you feel.

A new calm had begun to creep into my days, which was still surprising given what my life had become. All the things I thought brought security in the past had been shams. I felt more secure and free than ever before. After each session with Sean, new hope sprang forward. I could see it was a continuing path and I was learning how not to be discouraged when the next issue came up. In fact, it had become exciting - like finding that last piece of the jigsaw puzzle under the couch. Like a great mystery we were reading backwards. This was quite possibly the first time I'd moved forward with any real confidence in life.

Drifting into the cool, calming darkness of my subconscious during hypnotherapy made time seem almost imaginary. This portal into the past cast a glimmering hope that there was more to life than just the daily drama which seemed totally focused on money and appearance. Small things started to make more sense, things I couldn't help but notice. For years I'd held onto a book titled "There are No Accidents: Synchronicity and the Stories of Our Lives". I'd drug it around from place to place and now I was starting to see why. There was purpose in all things.

I read a lot and made loads of trips to the library, dividing my time between that and the big black trash can which was still in the picture. It was like one big investigation which was something I had loved as far back as high school. We had a pair of married teachers, the Echols. One taught home economics, the other photography and journalism.

Because my mom had an ancient sewing machine, the kind with the giant foot pedal, I knew how to sew. And as electives went, home ec. seemed like a safe bet. I liked Mrs. Echols so I was curious about her husband. I wasn't all that great in English, but I was really curious about photojournalism, so I signed up for the yearbook class that Mr. Echols taught.

A few weeks into the semester, after some sort of

ridiculous unanimous vote, I'd been named the editor of the yearbook in my senior year. These people were fools if they thought I knew what I was doing! I was pretty certain there was just no one else who wanted to do it, but it was also very nice to be selected rather than feeling left out as usual.

Again, I ran headfirst into a bunch of expectations I had no idea what to do with. Mr. Echols kept aggressively hinting at things that an editor should be doing. This would have been a great time for him to step up and teach me how to edit the thing.

How it became my life that others continually assumed I knew things I'd not been taught I have no idea. Somehow the heavens above seemed to have cast an invisible flashing neon sign reading "don't prepare her" over my forehead. The angels must have been laughing at me as I fumbled about my life, like I was a character on I Love Lucy.

As we ran the layouts and reviewed the copy we needed more photos, and I was sent out to do the job. For the first time I felt like I had found my groove in something I actually liked to do and had chosen for myself. Finally, I felt accepted and was hopeful for the future. I was excited to share my newfound passion with my parents.

I wanted to become a photojournalist. The idea of getting out there in life and not only learning what was happening around us but sharing it with words and pictures sounded incredible, like it was made for me. But there was Dad, face snarled up, looking at me sideways, like he couldn't wait to burst another dream for me. He told me that it was a dying business, and I was crazy to want to do that. The foundationless child I'd become was defeated by those words, too vulnerable to know better.

Just a few weeks later I'd find myself in another disappointing confrontation with an older man. Mr. Echols angrily took me aside in class and asked why I hadn't been at the senior class awards ceremony the previous evening. My reasoning was simple: I couldn't think of one award that would have been coming my way. Then he handed me the award I'd earned as yearbook editor. I was shocked and to this day, it's the only award I've won in my life.

CHAPTER 18: ORIGINS

The core root of it all will be found in childhood but only if you are willing to look there.

As my possessions were shrinking, my mind kept expanding. It became easier to notice myself and what I was doing. I concentrated on my behavior when it came to food and had begun collecting bundles of clues on a note pad which I'd carry with me into Sean's office.

With each visit we began in an easy exchange, me narrating the latest hurdles, Sean pointing out connections, careful to make sure I was understood. He'd then dimmed the lights a bit, queued up some background music, and I began to relax. Deeply inhaling fresh clean energy, releasing negativity with each exhale. Sean wouldn't offer suggestions. As I let myself go deeply into my subconscious, set before me each time was the backdrop of shadowy storm clouds, threatening the peace of the ocean's allure at dusk. I could feel my feet upon the cool sand awaiting an incoming storm. Through the roar of the waves Sean's voice would come along with me, keeping me safe as he guided me to relax different parts of my body while my mind began sinking further into my subconscious. Finally, he'd ask me to find myself at the top of that familiar staircase.

Following a dark slate set of stairs in the sand, I descended into a cave that was a bit grim from the onset. Attentive to Sean's voice, I felt myself dropping deeper into relaxation with each step until finally I found the last five where I was to count backwards and with each double my relaxation. At the bottom again I found the door and described it in detail. With each visit the door changed and sometimes there was no door at all.

On this particular day the door was foreboding and difficult to move. Once I found my way in, I saw a perfectly black void, filled with such cold dampness it sent chills down my spine. At the very top right I noticed a miniscule glimmer of brightness. In near panic I could hear Sean's voice calling from afar, asking if I could walk farther on to find someone to help, but I felt immobilized surrounded by the heavy air.

Voices began to seep through in choppy sentences. My parents' were fighting. In the openness of the cave, it seemed impossible to feel more constricted, yet I was. A feeling of being physically threatened abruptly washed over me, filling me with terror. I thought for a moment I might be sick. Sean asked if I wanted to come back, but I couldn't. I had to hear what was being said. They were talking about hurting me, but I couldn't understand why. Suddenly the pain erupted along with a deluge of tears, and my gasping for air. I sobbed until I felt the pain release me. As I calmed down and became more aware of my adult self, again able to connect with logic, all I could do was face the facts.

That conversation had been about aborting me. When Sean finally brought me back to the surface we started putting the pieces together. For years claustrophobia had left me feeling that small tight spaces meant death and of course not all of them did. Later, as more came to the surface we'd tie this into the feelings of being unwanted. I'd weathered the storm of this visit, but the forecast was for a gloomy week ahead as I processed those memories. My reluctance to go all in on relationships or to fully be vulnerable with anyone had begun right there, the very first moment the trust of my parents was broken.

It's true we can never fully know anyone else's story, but we also don't know just how much of our own can be hidden. At least not until we become willing (or are shoved) to take time to uncover what lurks in the shadows of our past. Our lives, perceptions and beliefs are products of our experiences. What my parents experienced that had laid the groundwork for this was taken to the grave with them. In many ways I'd like to think it less complicated to understand the behavior of my father than mother. His background seemed to explain a little more as well as add some intrigue. Dad's parents were Russian Germans who had immigrated to South Dakota.

It wasn't until I had to round up some documents for my father's funeral in January 1990 that I stumbled upon that interesting bit of my heritage. When I glanced over my dad's birth certificate I learned both of my grandparents had been born in Russia. I thought I was half German because that's what I'd been told. I couldn't help but wonder if this had the same shame tied to it as my parents' anniversary. My family seemed to wear shame like an anchor. I had to wrap my head around that lie and how I felt about being half Russian.

Recently when I sleuthed a bit deeper I found my father's hometown in South Dakota had been heavily occupied with people who were considered Germans but had lived in Russia for centuries, many of whom had immigrated at the turn of the century in the 1800s to the States. I'd also learned a bit about the German migration to Russia back in the 1700s under the helm of Catherine the Great.

Dad was one of eleven children born in 1905 and heavily impacted by the Great Depression. For someone who had longed for more family mine was not one that was terribly tight knit. My uncle Don lived the closest, so we saw him the most. Still, only a handful of times. Aunts Marie and Katie had visited once or twice from the Midwest and the rest I'd not laid eyes on.

Marie and Katie had kept in touch with me but that would be another thing destroyed by my father. While creating her will, Marie let him know she intended to include a gift of five thousand dollars for me. In my mid-twenties when she left us, I certainly could have used that money. But, in his usual fashion my dad forbade it because he was a racist and I was dating a black man. He was so bitter he'd stopped talking to me for years.

He had been so petty he had even stopped me from going to Grad Nite at Disneyland because I wanted to go with a black friend. What a shitty thing to do to two kids in high school. I will never forget the look on my friends face when I told him, the absolute most embarrassing thing I could do to him, all because of conditioned stupidity. Eddie Smith, I am forever humbly sorry to have been that person in your life.

My mom's side of the family fortunately was more accepting and seemed closer to each other, but I think she may have been somewhat of an outcast or the black sheep of the bunch. Of her two brothers and two sisters, she was the least stable, having been married 4 times and abandoning her own child from her third marriage. I was not surprised the day my great aunt had told me my mom always needed a little more help.

That same great aunt was my number one fan. We were so close I called her Grandma Gert. She was the sister of my actual grandma, Grace, and lived the closest to us in Las Vegas on a street called Hickey (of all things). She was a straight-shooting, no-nonsense woman who stood up most of the time because she thought it was healthier than sitting. A woman before her time! She did two things I was incredibly grateful for: she rarely failed to call out either of my parents on their less-than-stellar parenting while doing all she could for me. As a child she took time and care to be sure that each gift from her was personal to me; a charm bracelet with a baby shoe bearing my name and birthdate, or a bath towel with my name embroidered on it.

Through time I'd come to notice the comments she'd make on my behalf with each of my parents, whether to caution how they spoke with me or to care more about my personal development. But she hadn't really explained why a woman who prided herself on being like Rosie the Riveter in the shipyards of Long Beach could walk away from her eleven-year-old son or neglect her daughter to the degree she had with me.

We visited Grandma Gert and her husband Grampa Bob a lot because it meant my parents could drink, smoke, gamble and have fun, all with a free place to stay. One visit when I was around ten was exciting for me too. Circus Circus Hotel and Casino had just opened and was the first to offer something for kids.

As we entered, the bustling casino at the Circus Circus was cramped with exuberant people. Someone, (I can't swear who exactly) had even given me some money to go play the games on the kids' level. It was a big deal for me to be left on my own. From the upper vantage I settled along a rail overlooking the casino. As slot machines zinged, and clanged, sputtering out coins, lights of all colors splashed across the floor, ceiling, and walls. Trapeze artists and dazzling tight-wire acts performed right at my eye level as I stood vigilantly watchful, timidly mesmerized! After the show I cautiously chose a game or two and tried my luck, unexpectedly winning and getting a momentary taste of happiness.

I walked, head held high with pride, clutching a red fuzz covered plastic bull about the size of puppy. I had to show someone, and Grandma Gert was the first person I saw, She was beaming with delight for me, repeating sweetly how much she loved my prize! We were both so happy I held it out to her without hesitation, wanting her to have it since she loved it so much. It was my first chance to do something for the one adult who had really taken the time to see me as an individual.

Brilliantly, as if she'd known my heart would be broken if she refused, she accepted her gift and hugged me tightly. It was such a sweet, loving, and validating moment. Nothing like anything I'd felt before. I wanted my mom to see me, to appreciate my win and my gift. But when we found her she just looked sad. There was a frown on her face. She said she wanted the bull. She wished I'd given it to her instead. My heart sank. My wonderful grandma offered, but Mom refused, saying I hadn't wanted her to have it. What had begun as an exciting adventure and led to my first moments of real pride were crushed by my mom's lack of emotional awareness. She seemed to have an unending cache of ways to break me down.

All I could do was soak it in. When I glance through old photos the painful feeling of being an outsider, of being so different from anyone else, like a giant blob in everyone's way in my own family still makes me cringe. And my face reflected those feelings in the images.

There was just such a large n u m b e r of jabs thrown in my direction. Slashes of unkindness, impossible to shield myself from, especially with no support or help in understanding the pain and fear. There were the small things like having to learn the basics from my teachers such as how to tie my shoes, cover my mouth when coughing or to sit with my legs crossed when wearing a dress. They added to the daily doses of neglect and disrespect at home combined to minimize and demean me. It seems a child's psyche can be verbally stabbed into submission.

I was about four the first time I remember my half-brother Barry visiting. He was eleven years older than me and had been assigned to babysit while my parents went out. I was so little and innocent I probably expected to have fun, but all the fun that night was meant for Barry. He was tuned into his favorite TV show and had one of those three packs of Cracker Jacks. He pointed to the red tape holding the three boxes together and asked me if I knew what it was, of course I had no idea. Blood, he said and then told me if I happened to end up bleeding that night he'd have to save that blood so it could be used to make more tape. Gross.

But that wasn't enough for him. His second act opened after the phone rang. He hung up saying he had bad news; both my parents had just died in a car accident. I was four. I kid you not, this is what he thought was funny for a small child. Before he could get his laughs in, he first had to explain to me what death was, and even took time to make up a gruesome story with details of the crash. I ran screaming into my bedroom where I remained sobbing until my parents returned.

He wasn't the only boy in my family who thought I was fair game for cruel pranks. A few years after that we were visiting mom's sister, Peggy, and her family who lived in a lovely, wooded neighborhood up north. They shared stories of life in Alaska when Uncle Bob had been stationed there in the Air Force. He spoke of the little private plane he owned with joy that I'd not seen on a man's face before. They had two elegant daughters much older than I, slender, well mannered, and stylish in their attire. But their younger brother, Bobby was closer to my age, so we were told to go outside and play.

I was excited to be on this new adventure. There were real trees, not the dry monstrous cacti that surrounded my house. Everything was green. The forest was cool and damp. Bobby and I traveled down a well-worn path together until we veered off the trail. Bobby said he wanted to go to his friend's house and kept walking through the woods away from the trail. We'd gone quite a distance when his pace accelerated. I have a sneaking suspicion he'd planned this from the start.

What he did next was the stuff of parents worst nightmares. Well, depending on who your parents are, I guess. My cousin left me alone there in the woods. He mumbled something like I should just turn back and then took off running. I couldn't keep up with him and he wasn't listening to me. I had no idea which way to go.

Hot tears streamed down my face as I searched but no path appeared. I have no idea how long I stood in that forest crying but it was long enough that I had finally stopped screaming. Bobby had been able to lead my uncle to find me where I sat on the ground, trembling while Bobby got his ass handed to him by his dad.

It's the accumulation of these types of experiences that shape us going forward. When trust is broken so often by so many, when it seems like you matter less and less as time goes on, those subtle messages that wash over you like a scalding shower set the tone for who you become as an adult. Trauma is trauma, no matter how it happens. It all slides in through the days as they pass, amassing, forming our beliefs without us giving it any thought. It's just imposed upon us by the actions of others and molds how we behave. Having fun for me was ruined in those moments because I had learned there were few I could trust. But I'd have to unearth the pain to release the understanding and change how I felt.

My uncle had been railing on my cousin on the walk home and was already heading through the door when my aunt took over. My parents sat there, as did I. The fuss was made over the squeaky wheel, who was my cousin. Maybe they made him apologize, I'm not sure, but no one asked how I was feeling. They just kept telling me I was okay. Was I? When it repeatedly seems as if no one actually cares that you are ok, it sends a message that you shouldn't care if you are either. These are the experiences that linger and cause the triggers central to obsessive and dysfunctional behavior. They also make me wonder how I never went insane.

CHAPTER 19: WAS THERE LIFE OUTSIDE CALIFORNIA?

*Sometimes to take full responsibility for
your life you must do a lot of sorting.*

Like the curtains being thrown back after a long tedious winter, light continued to pour into my life. With Sean's help I learned that my dad had done more harm to my psyche than my mom ("Man, your dad was a bad dude"). Gradually the burden of things that I had no responsibility for shifted onto those who did. There were times during a visit with Sean where I'd feel anger toward my father. But once in the subconscious I had all I needed to both fix and release that old, stale pain. It's a lot like being right there in it but not feeling the need to take it so personally.

At the start of 2014 I'd been talking to William about

moving to his area. He said it was alright with him and even that it might be nice to have me closer. So, I started getting more serious about clearing out the house.

I'd once read that most people don't move any further than two hundred miles from their hometown, which had been true of me. California was the only state I'd ever lived in, and this was going to be the biggest thing I'd ever chosen to do in my life.

After months of having no idea what I was doing, forming a plan felt a little weird but came together quicker than expected when one of my closest friends, Brad recommended a realtor. The next thing I knew, the house was on the market.

Which meant I had to get my shit together for perspective buyers. The house had huge gaps where furniture had once been and huge piles of stuff, all over the place, targeted for the driveway. And I had to talk with my son about all the boxes of his stuff he had stored in the garage rafters.

For a while it was like a new kind of shock. I'd wake up in cold sweats in the middle of the night, wondering what I had done. And everyone had an opinion. And felt comfortable sharing them. They were worried if I sold I'd not be able to afford to come back. The funny thing was, no one asked if I might want to.

Nita visited more often and would stand in my house wondering how much of my furniture she could fit into her house. I learned two things during this time. When you think you are down to the very last thing you can sell, you will still be able to sell at least half as much of what you have left. And don't listen to any realtor about what needs to be done to your house before you sell it. That would have saved me thousands of dollars.

The house was the last tie to my old way of life, the only way of life I'd understood before. And while most everyone around me disliked my departure from it all, somehow I just knew it was all going to be alright. Removing the focus from making money had been like opening the door to a room filled with light. The drive towards what I had once perceived as success had been replaced by peace. I knew a bigger plan was already in place, bigger than I would have made for myself.

Sean and I could continue our meetings over the phone. I hadn't found what I needed to lose any weight, but the work I was doing had become so much more important. And after several grueling months, William and I were in a better place again. I had a whole new life to look forward to, but I still had a lot to do to make that happen.

One warm evening I got on a call with my son and spent several hours in the garage sorting out those boxes. William's dad Keith and I lived on an Air Force base when he was born, and that first year when we were shopping for his gifts, we found a glass Christmas ornament that read "Baby's First Christmas" dated with the year. We had to have it. I then made it my solemn duty to collect at least one, if not more, ornaments each year thereafter. So, there we were, thirty-eight years later, talking about each one of them.

I was just at the beginning stage of understanding and accepting how adversely I'd affected William, so I probably wasn't prepared for what was about to happen. As we talked about each ornament, I saw a pattern emerging. William was far less interested in his collection than I was. I hadn't just bought mom type stuff; there were mostly awesome Star Wars, sports, and other guy-centric ornaments I thought he would love. He whacked it down to about a third.

Each holiday season I watch those Hallmark movies where the families cherish each ornament they hang, sharing stories of how they were collected. It's heartwarming, but not what I was experiencing in this moment. Selling those were my least favorite thing to be doing but out they went, a little piece of my heart with each. I'm not really sure why it is we expect people to be grateful for things they didn't ask for but it's an interesting concept isn't it?

That was a part of purging. And the layers of physical

stuff along with my own bullshit were being peeled back further each week. In every possible way I was making space so I could see what was really important. The beauty of doing this type of work is the movement forward. The obsessive times with food were more reasonable. The urgent need to be soothed was not as frequent or defining. Knowing I was doing the work was part of how I began to cope.

One great thing about that house was it has plenty of natural light and plants loved it there. There is something a bit nostalgic about seeing a once tiny plant found half-dead at Home Depot being taken to a new home, all six feet of it.

It was too getting real.

There were no offers on the house right away but one day I noticed a couple had been parked out front of the house for a while. I went to say hi. A few days later they came by with their realtor. And a few days after that they came by again with a structural engineer. This was enough to make my palms sweaty and cause a moment of panic. I'd been chatting with this couple, and they were great folks. The kind that would fit very well into the neighborhood, probably better than I had.

Finding the right fit was something I wanted to be cognizant of because my neighbors had earned that. Well, and some of them had been pretty vocal about my responsibility to do that as well! Sure enough, their offer arrived. I held the paperwork in my hands and sank to the floor. The last thirty years of my life had been spent in San Diego, the last ten in that house. It seemed impossible to believe, but it was time to let go. I would officially be willingly de-housed in thirty days.

Nita and I stood there in those last week's looking at the bareness around us. With each visit she was more astonished that I could make do with so little but now she was just shaking her head. I was using a wooden wine box for a table between the two recliners, the last of the furniture in the front of the house.

She stopped shaking her head long enough to stake her claim on those recliners. But before she took a sticky note to the TV, I told her I had already decided that would be going with me. This was back in the days when a nice TV and sound system cost big money, so yeah, it was going with me. I'd already found a moving company headed in the same direction, who was able to add our small amount of stuff to their trip.

On the very last weekend, Nita and I had one last garage sale! It seemed impossible but somehow we'd managed to sell every last thing I'd collected in fifty-five years. Nita and I disassembled the surround sound system, being careful to number each piece with painters' tape so I could make it work when setting it up again. She walked around and asked me what was going on with the desk and chair still in my office. I'd had it on Offer Up with no takers.

Early the next day the moving truck arrived, and I watched as they loaded up the eight boxes (half of which represented William's memories, the other half my entire life) along with the TV, and a Dyson vacuum (which I still use today). Nita had come to collect her new recliners and together we set the desk outside the house and posted it on Offer Up for free. I was happy that the new owners told me it was gone by the time they arrived.

And that was it. I was done with that house. I was done with life in California. I was done with the old way of doing things.

CHAPTER 20: FREE AS THE WIND

Releasing the illusion of control opens the flow of the universe.

That cool, crisp, beautiful morning, it was finally happening. After Nita and the movers left, I slowly walked through the now deserted house. It was my house no more. The only part of it I would actually miss was the patio. It had been such a great space. My neighbor Mike had extended the cover which made it great for outdoor entertaining. Those were the best of times there for me. We'd even held a memorial for Flap when he passed.

I closed my eyes and rested for a moment in the enormity of it all. No matter what happened from this day forward there would not be another move like this. This was symbolic. It was the full release of a broken reality that had been propped up by false beliefs and insecurities.

How do we do it? How is it possible to focus with total determination in the wrong direction for so long with great certainty that it's right?

I hadn't even come close to understanding how much I'd sacrificed for everything I was now leaving behind. None of the hard work that had gone into any of that had been for what I had truly needed. Even though it had all seemed like what I so desperately wanted. But nothing sooths childhood grief when it is so hidden, especially when we are so busy avoiding the pain and anxiety it has left us with.

Could I simply be wrong? I was certainly alone in my thought process. I didn't know anyone who was doing anything like this. My friends had somewhat adjusted to it, but no one was saying hey, that's a great idea and actively following suit.

There was nothing left to do then but finish up my goodbyes. I'd been doing my own adaptation of a farewell tour. San Diego had been home for thirty years and just enough people were interested in my departure to make me feel a bit like a rock star for a moment and it was wonderful. The send offs were deeply heartfelt. So many of these friends had become the family I'd longed for. Getting to visit with them took on an all-new meaning now. Gone was the rushed feeling of having too much to do to really listen, in its place a new calm. My life was being reordered and my priorities were aligning.

When it came close to time for me to hit the road for real

(and I no longer had a bed), one of the last nights had been spent in Gerard's guest room. He'd given me a card filled with more sentiment than I'd heard from him in all the years I'd known him, and we were both teary as I drove away.

Up until then I'd been able to avoid social media which was one more thing my friends disliked. How would they know that I was safe they wondered. And even though I'd gotten a complete tune up of both my car and my health I knew they had a point. So, I promised to start a blog to prove I was still alive and share what I was doing. To this day, Leaving San Diego is still out there showing many of the details of my trip.

As I hopped into the driver's seat for the last time in my old garage I closed my eyes in celebration and thanks. I had been beyond fortunate in so many ways. I backed out of the driveway and headed to the bank, not looking back. The only direction I wanted to see was forward.

And for the first time it hit me, a brand-new emotion. The absolute joy of freedom. Other than making sure my cell phone and health insurance bills were paid I had zero responsibilities for the foreseeable future. Something about leaving nearly every single material possession behind opened the world's doors to me. The air felt better, I could breathe deeper, I was more excited than I'd ever been in my life. As I drove down the street all the complications of life, and all the daily drama gave way to an indescribable newfound feeling of peace. Any shred of doubt blew right out my open windows.

I hadn't been back up to Washington to find a place and set it up. To be honest I just wasn't worried about that at all. My most recent experiences were teaching me that things would fall into place. For example, there had been a time when I had considered renting my house and gotten all the way to the day the lease was to be signed. For some reason I just couldn't do it, which in the end turned out to be the best thing that could have happened.

So many people have shared that they thought my actions were incredibly brave, which I appreciated. But to me it felt less brave and more guided or directed. It was the beginning of a bit of balance. An awareness of the importance of ourselves internally, and a new openness to spirituality. And a better knowledge about the havoc that happens when we are out of touch with any of those components. I had lived a life of havoc and it was time to remedy that. I was moving into something more. The days of living a life I had not chosen and living by default were over.

 A really divine thing happened during the pandemic. I'd had a library book to return but had not made it before everything was closed. I'd had the book so long I forgot what it even was or why I hadn't read it. After months of it sitting in my car I turned it over to discover it was the same book that had been coming up everywhere in my life. Every time I turned around I'd see this book mentioned. And it ended up being the most important book out of all I'd read titled the Untethered Soul.

This has continued for years now. Things come into my life without any effort on my part and no rituals of manifestation. No joke. I needed an extension cord, there was one in the parking lot at Starbucks. I thought about getting some bigger pots for some plants, when out for a walk there were a half dozen outside someone's fence on the sidewalk. I wanted a small dish rack, walking down the alley there was one in the recycle bin. Same with a mirror, chairs, firewood, a dishpan and so on. Just before I started writing this someone gifted me a year's subscription to Masterclass, and I've been able to watch courses by prominent authors. Just yesterday when I was at the beach with a friend when I wondered out loud if I should get an extra beach chair and as we were walking home not two minutes later we found a perfectly good one in the alley. After all this time, being unafraid and open minded has not failed me yet and my road trip was to become a great beginning to an amazing adventure.

CHAPTER 21: WELCOME TO LALALAND

Adventures are the sweetest when friendships are rekindled.

I was heading in the direction of Los Angeles and had contacted three old friends who lived there, a chef, an actor and a photographer. I was hoping to catch up in person and prayed they lived close to each other because when it comes to driving in California, Los Angeles is the worst. There is almost no good time to find yourself on the road there.

I've had some great trips to LA but, I've also had a rough trip there for a funeral. I'd just begun dating a guy who lived there but worked in San Diego, and we had plans to meet in L.A. for a Laker game. We both had to work the day of the game. Rich, my date, had called three times saying he wanted to come see me that day. I didn't understand since we'd be seeing each other that night and I wanted to finish my work so I could leave. With each call, after I confirmed he was coming to the game, I said I'd just see him then.

After leaving Rich's ticket at will-call, I grabbed a beer and settled in for the excitement of both the game and our date. This was before cell phones so all I could do was cheer on the team and wait to see Rich's smiling face. By half-time I was seriously worried. Rich never made it.

That night he was killed in a head on car crash just one block from his house. Rich's cousin let me know about the funeral, but no one seemed to know what happened. Maybe I would have known if I'd taken the time to see him as he'd asked. Whatever he wanted to tell me went to the grave with him. It still haunts me, especially when I go to Los Angeles.

The first visit on the road trip kicked off at a restaurant called Café Med somewhere in the downtown LA area. I met with an old work buddy, Jared, and his wife. Jared was an energetic entrepreneur who had already successfully opened two restaurants on his own. It was great to be able to catch up and hear all the future plans for the restaurant they were creating together. The evening had been lovely, we shared a great meal and some fabulous cocktails. I was happy for them and feeling happy myself. Around ten p.m. the day had caught up with me and I was tired as I scrambled to find a place to stay. My first night as a purposefully de-homed person was spent at a reasonably priced Ramada Inn somewhere in the middle of LaLaLand.

On day two I caught up with my friend Remy at Sweet Butter café. We stayed so long that we had to exchange our breakfast menus and coffee for lunch and cocktails! Remy and I had known each other for close to twenty years so four hours just flew by. When she left San Diego she rebased herself in not so sunny Seattle for photography school and had become so successful she had decided to move her brand to Los Angeles. We chatted about her latest projects and my new adventure. A lot of laughs, pictures, and hugs later we promised to keep in better touch and went back to the stories of our own lives, which sent me in search of an Airbnb for the night.

In West Hollywood I ended up sharing an apartment with a couple of very busy filmmakers. Weaving my way through heaps and piles of equipment amid brief greetings I managed to find out they were working on the movie Like You Mean It which eventually made it all the way through production. Ironically at the top of the movie poster the words - **Love...Feel...Hurt...Live** - would end up the exact theme of my journey over the upcoming few years.

Around nine that night, I headed over to a place called

Magnolia on Sunset Blvd. and Vine, which was Walk-of-Fame adjacent, to find my charming friend Antonio already ordering a cocktail. We hugged like the long-lost friends we were and sat outside watching the crazies go by talking about where life had taken us both. As we were discussing how much he'd enjoyed his role in the latest Oliver Stone film I thought back on some of our talks and how far he'd come. It was such a blessing to see. Two days before, I had no clue where life would take me and the next thing you know I'm sitting in Hollywood having a late-night bite with a movie star. Antonio has since gone on to do some very interesting and incredible work, but he's stayed as humble and true to himself as the very first day I met him all those years ago. And every time I see him he still looks embarrassed when someone recognizes him.

By the end of day two I felt well settled into life on the road and quite comfortable haphazardly placing myself in the beds of strangers by night. My friends in LA held up their end of bargain by thoroughly entertaining me and the one thing they all had in common was that they all hated living there. The grind is the grind no matter where you are, I guess.

Day three I got in the car wondering if having no direction in mind was at all deranged. I decided what really felt insane was that I had nowhere at all to be. Nothing had any bearing on my timeline or direction, and it was glorious. If something looked provocative I stopped. If another driver was being too much of a buffoon I simply pulled over. Being stuck in that past lifestyle for so long had made this possible, but the real gratitude came from getting out from under it and not falling in line with the beliefs that it needed to be perpetuated.

I made a stop for gas and the man behind the counter told me to make sure I tried the legendary scones at a renowned local café and bakery. So, I settled in on the charming little outdoor patio chatting with the lovely staff, trying out the scones with no idea where I was. Somewhere on the west coast north of LA. I'd been keeping a little journal of my spending, so I logged this meal. I thought it might be fun to know how much the trip cost in the end. Money was still something I needed to work on and being on the road reminded me of something that had traumatized me on a different road trip.

I was still in high school when Keith and my parents took a trip to Vegas. My dad had randomly handed me a five-dollar bill. As far as I can remember this was the first time I'd been given any cash that wasn't earmarked for something because I sure as shit didn't get an allowance. We had stopped halfway on the trip. Keith and I had been looking around a small shop when I spotted a turquoise ring that I not only liked but could pay for on my own.

I was so excited. We regrouped to discuss where to have lunch when my dad said lunch should be my treat since he knew I had money. I stared up in his eyes and saw him looking at my hand. He'd set me up for failure and made sure to do it in front of Keith. What a dick move. Character assassination; just one of the thousands of tiny cuts to my psyche as a kid.

I wound my way up the coast to Santa Barbara and spotted a cute yet dive-ish looking wine bar which screamed my name. The owner was impressively knowledgeable about the selections she offered and still as down to earth as a neighbor you'd love having. As she poured my third glass it seemed like finding a place to stay should happen sooner than later. Scrolling Airbnb, I stumbled upon a guest house right up the road that looked quiet and quaint.

The first Airbnb in LA was surrounded by the makings of a movie. Here I felt like I was the star of my own show. The home was a sprawling ranch style with terracotta tiles and custom interiors. The beauty of the neighborhood and the charm of the location brought about a feeling of warmth and richness. There was a solidness here like a bastion of safety, a haven protecting those who found their way to it. It was unforgettable, I slept like a freaking log and hated to leave. I thought about lounging around for another night, but this felt too much like one of those places where you go for a visit and end up staying a lifetime. And I had another visit in mind, so I made my way to Paso Robles for my next stop.

Avila beach was beautiful, my gracious hosts were good company and fun tour guides who invited me for an overnight visit. Considering I didn't know this couple well as they were family of friends it was quite a treat. After a bit of exploring the local caves we enjoyed some delightful local wine to go along with a fine meal. The next day I set off on my own again to try out the local vineyards. Apparently my road trip was turning into a wine tasting tour and from the likes of Tobin James, Eberle, Robert Hall, and Tomas Hill Organics, the evidence was there; these guys knew what they were doing. And Tobin James, the man himself, is hella funny once you get him talking! Before I got too hammered I left wine country to spend the night at Pismo Beach. And one more night of excellent sleep with the ocean breeze blowing through my open window gave way to a deeper peace and an odd sense that somehow anything was possible.

I didn't have a lot of experience waking up so close to the ocean so breathing in the Pismo Beach salt air so early was excellent. I grabbed my cell phone and took a walk, in search of coffee while dialing my friends Brad and Tiffany. When I told them where I was the told me to come visit them too!

I love that Brad considers me his second mom; it's an amazing honor. He's also one of the few people that I vividly remember the exact moment when we met. It had been in 2000 during a mass hiring event while opening a new location. Brad had breezed in very nonchalantly with his girlfriend, who was applying for a job. I'm sure he thought he was just there for support and was surprised when he found himself sitting in front of an application! If he wanted to perch himself in my chair I told him he needed to get that filled out. He grinned and told me no; he had a job already. I handed him a pen. He tried to speak, but I raised one eyebrow and gave a stern enough look that he started writing. I'm pretty sure it was illegal. All I knew was he needed to work for us.

The next day I called him and said if he wanted his girlfriend to have the job he had to come along, which I'm certain was illegal. I pretty much begged him to work just one day a week. My instincts were right or more likely it had been fate. He ended up staying six years longer than the girlfriend and he credits the experience for helping shape his life. For me, the best part was I got a great friend, not to mention a first-rate employee. I even gained another soulmate in the amazing Tiffany, who he later chose to be his wife. During the entire time my journey unfolded, Tiffany was on board with each and every crazy thing I did. And to everyone's delight, Brad is an amazing cook and sommelier.

CHAPTER 22: SOMETHING WAS BREWING

The components of a great beer are both as easy and as complex as that of a great friendship.

When you are a lover of craft beer the idea of moving away from San Diego makes about as much sense as buying a bikini for a snowstorm, yet this was what I had done. The thing about the San Diego brew scene was-at that time it was almost obscure. People outside the city often think of just a few heavy hitters without knowing there are far more craft breweries per capita in San Diego than anywhere in the U.S. And those brewers were social in a way that made you want to be one of them. There was a comradery. Not a hundred percent, there were a few snobs but for the most part it had become a well-run, kick ass community.

And then I left. And found it's a whole lot different

elsewhere. So, one fine day during my stay that turned out to be almost a weeklong, Brad and I put on our game faces and took a tour of all the breweries within a half hour of his home. There were four. Our mistake was starting at Knee Deep because it was impressive enough to set the bar too high. When we bellied up at the next place, we instantly ordered the sampler boards like boss bitches. We were full of compliments, the place looked great, the beers sounded amazing, the beer tender was fun and friendly. And then we took the first sips of our tasters.

Eyes wide, we gave each other a sideways glance, with wrinkled up noses. It was like a skunk must have been let lose in the hop fields. The beer from this brewery was nowhere near the tasty quality of our first stop and considering beer usually gets better the more you drink we got worried. Getting up from a dozen or more nearly full taster glasses is something you will rarely see either of us do but we took our leave with lots of beer left on the bar. The next two did not make things better. The good news is over the years we've returned to them all and each are now phenomenal. But back then I was still looking for good beer! So, before I took off, Brad told me I had to stop at Russian River and Bear Republic.

Somewhere around the two week mark I started back toward the coast and rambled along scenic Highway One. On this dynamic path you'll find huge expanses of land where you might see cows grazing on one side of the road as the waves of the Pacific crash just a few feet away on the other. There is a cove that is home to the largest formation of sea lions on the west coast which was quite a site and very noisy! A few miles up the road you will find the most expensive gas in the nation, it was triple the cost of what I had paid the day before. And somehow I found myself having lunch with an incredibly famous old doowop singer and his wife after chatting away at the bar.

What would be next? Well, another day of drinking!

Russian River brewery is housed in a somewhat nondescript building. With great anticipation I stepped in and wondered if I'd missed the brewery and walked into a dive bar instead. That's the problem with being familiar with only one type of brew scene. The bar was jam packed, but I was able to squeeze onto a stool and there I sat. And sat. And sat some more. I began to seriously wonder if I'd become invisible. And I was in the center of the bar! When I finally flagged down the server, he looked indignant. Clearly it was my privilege to be there. Lunch and a few tasters later I snaped a selfie in my Societie hoodie (a hometown brewery favorite) and posted it on my blog. The food and beer had been great, but this brewery was so well known it had kind of outgrown the location. I had been there and that was what counted the most. Sometimes it's just about showing up and taking those punches.

Bear Republic brought a much better experience. I had to try their award-winning Racer 5 and a few other samples. After having a great time, I snapped another shot for my blog which was getting some attention by the beer world back home. By now I'd learned to sample very lightly and keep expectations to a minimum, so I felt confident I could make one more tour in Healdsburg for a tasting at Seghesio winery. Even though I'd had less than two beers and what equaled a half a glass of wine I soon I suspected I might be on my way to an Alcoholic Anonymous meeting...but holy hell, how could I do another anything anonymous meeting ever again.

The next stop was for coffee and water so I could set out for Eureka California which sits about a hundred miles outside the Oregon border. My buddy Chuck (of squirrel gun fame) had told me about a must try a brewery there and I would have flown right past this little town if not. With the sightseeing as limited as the Airbnb options I grabbed a room in a hotel which could have passed for a motel instead...but I had a fresh place to stay, and I was happy. Eureka would be my last foreseeable night in California which was a strange thing to even think about.

I thought about all the friends I'd just left behind, especially Chuck since he was the reason I was in Eureka. He is simply a blessing. Chuck has the rare ability to be kind yet honestly present all the time. At that time, it was hard to imagine how he pulled that off, but it's been close to thirty years since we met, and he's been consistently the same since day one.

Chuck started out on my team at the first location, and I instantly loved him. One day he strolled into my office, plopped himself down, and told me he'd met the girl of his dreams. I smiled thinking it was infatuation, but as the days passed, he was more and more certain he had found the one. So, as a fun challenge (or a favor in case he was right) I asked what he had planned for an engagement ring. He said something like...well, I don't know so, in another first, I offered to set up a savings plan. Which may also have been illegal. When the account balance was where he wanted it Chuck was ready to pop the question.

I have to say, Chuck is no slouch, but the girl of his dreams is drop dead gorgeous so I was a tiny bit worried for my friend as to how this would play out. The answer was a resounding YES! And, nearly thirty years later they are still together along with two amazingly brilliant, kind, and sweet kids, a Labrador, and a house by the beach. Chuck had taken the money and the time to go out and commission a custom ring for his loved one, which she is still wearing today.

As I write and we find ourselves drifting in and out of quarantine and unable to meet, I send him these pages via email, and he texts me if I get behind on his reading material. Along with Nita he's become a sincere partner on this writing excursion; and I feel incredibly blessed. Each with different perspectives but both so kind and open about what they are reading, telling me when I've left them confused and or what works well. And I'm caught off guard when they share how surprised they are about what I'd gone through, especially in my childhood. Chuck has said more than once that he wonders how I turned out "so normal". I still wonder about that myself.

That next morning, stretching cozily, a bit unwilling to step out of bed for that last day in Cali, I slowly showered, dressed, packed the car, and headed over to Lost Coast Brewery for food and drink. It was just small and divey enough to feel right at home which made me very happy. The friendly server didn't miss a beat and helped me navigate their award-winning beer list which was then paired with a brew made for another wonderful meal. Best of all, I wish I could send these stories filled with food and drink to my first-grade teacher, which makes for an appropriate end to California.

CHAPTER 23: HELLO OREGON!

Sometimes avoidance isn't about denial, sometimes it's about just staying sane.

As I stood from the warm wooden table next to the sunny window in the front of Lost Coast Brewery, the bill had been paid and it was time to get back to the road trip. The fact that I had no idea what life would bring made me wonder, was this truly the end of my being a Californian? Everything about me was starting to feel different. In front of me was a whole new state to traverse and unlike California, my choice of direction had more to do with who I didn't want to see than who I did. The current route would take me straight through the town where I believed my half-brother Barry still lived.

While it may feel good and even normal to walk away from a bad situation, there's something about the way those memories can stay with us. Some seem tucked away in dark shrouded corners, hiding dank mysteries that gives you chills when you try to peek in. My brother landed in one of those corners in my mind about twenty-five years ago, which was the last time that I saw him. All my thoughts about him had morphed over the years. As a small child he served as my own personal terrorist. As a teen my long-haired hippy idol. As an adult, let's just say… well, just miss me on that, which was exactly what I intended to do. What happened within my family was a tragedy of omission. Passive, aggressive omission. With Barry and I becoming the pawns.

It was an arduous and stressful time, when last I'd seen him. My dad had just passed away. My mom called me and said he was in bad shape, and I should hurry to get there. So, there I was driving like a completely insane person scared to death at what I might find but totally unprepared to see the body bag holding my dad being loaded in the back of the coroner's car as I arrived.

My dad was eighty-four when he died but my mom was in no way ready for it; she was very lost at being alone. I stayed there as long as I could. Her sister, Gwen, had come to stay for an extended period. But who mom really seemed to want was Barry, she even resorted to bribery to get him to visit.

I'd already spent two weeks in the high desert with my mom, staring down those blasted Joshua trees that had assaulted me as a kid. I was happy that both my brother and my aunt were there. Heading home the hot rancid air gave way to a cooler, saltier version with a bit of dampness, as the Joshuas were replaced with palms. My shoulders relaxed as the car coasted along on cruise control. Mom should be good for a bit, and it was time to get my own life back together.

Barry and Aunt Gwen weren't in town for more than a few days when my phone rang. I'd held some hope in my heart that these visits would bring some healing for our disjointed family, so I happily took the call. But in the background was a deep moaning, overshadowing Barry's request that I come home. Again.

My mom, who if you remember had just lost her husband, had fallen on the cement floor in the garage, a full twenty-four hours earlier.

The first thing that comes to my mind when a woman in her mid-seventies falls - is a broken hip. So, I asked what I thought was a normal question; why hadn't they called an ambulance. Barry yelled out to our mother asking if she wanted an ambulance, to which she said no. NO? I don't know why I didn't call one myself. Instead, they insisted I make the two-hour drive to take her to the hospital.

Mind blown...

How is it that three fully grown people - each one of them much older than me could not take care of an extreme emergency like this. They all had drivers' licenses and there was at least two running vehicles there. The entire drive I was fuming. When I arrived, my brother carried our mom to my tiny car (a two door Mazda mx6), crammed her inside, amid full blown screeching, while everyone acted like it was a normal day. Even though no one would take her, they all still wanted to come along. I strained to hold the driver's seat up to make room so my aunt and six-foot six brother could fold into the cramped back of the car. Off we went to the hospital, hillbilly style.

After the staff extracted mom and took her inside, Barry kept saying there was no way she'd broken her hip. My aunt swung between shaking her head and going outside for a smoke. I just sat like a deer in headlights wondering what I was supposed to do with this whole motley crew. My dad was gone, my mom was broken, and this was what I was left to work with.

My brother did an excellent job of looking shocked when the doctor told us what I already knew. Honestly, I'm surprised someone didn't report all of us for elder abuse. When we were finally allowed in to see her, she insisted that I be the one to help her into a gown instead of the nurse. It was like a scene from a movie. I felt so out of place. Not once in life had I seen her in a state of undress or in such vulnerability. A few years later, when I read "Tuesdays with Morrie," I thought of that moment and wished my mom could have been more like Morrie.

Her hospital stay would be two weeks long, which gave Aunt Gwen a reason to escape the lunacy that was our house. Barry had other plans.

While I had called a friend to come stay with me to help sort out some things to make Mom's return a bit brighter, Barry called a friend in to see what stuff of my dad's they could sell and make themselves some money. My friend and I cleaned, painted, and freshened up the place. As I did laundry Barry assumed I'd do his too. Covered in paint and dirt, Barry also assumed I'd be making dinner. And when the weekend rolled around he wanted to know

what clubs were good in town. He seemed to think it was a freaking money-making party zone and I was the maid. It was a rough two weeks.

When mom came home from the hospital he immediately shifted his focus. In short order he packed up the only antique quilt we had which was handmade by our grandmother along with the only copies of original family photos and took off the next day in my dad's van, another thing my mom had given him. Now, all this time later I realize my mom's very fragile and vulnerable state may have been the beginning of her own awareness of sorts. Or, perhaps more likely, without my dad she finally wanted her kids as allies.

Barry never returned again. My sister-in-law called right after he left to get my version of the events and that was the last time she and I spoke. Four years later when our mom had passed away, I had to call Barry because she'd left him five-thousand dollars (the same amount my aunt wanted to leave me). After I told him that she was gone all he said was "well?".

"Well, what?" I asked. Did he want to know what happened with our mom? Would he care how my young son and I had found her lifeless body? No, he asked nothing other than "How much?". He only wanted to know how much money she'd left behind for him. And that was the last time we spoke. I imagine having a mom leave you as an eleven-year-old boy to go raise another family is as horrifying as it sounds so this was likely the result. It still sucked.

I veered inland toward Bend, Oregon. I knew my brother had come by his particular style of behavior just as I had my own and was well aware that the choices our mom had made had affected both of us in such tragically differing ways. But I was not interested in stirring those turbulent waters. Bend was known for its breweries and that sounded far healthier to me.

My first stop was at a little place called Three Creeks Brewing in a town called Sisters. As long as it wasn't named Brothers I was game! Sisters and Three Creeks were so country cute. The entrance to the brewery looked like an A frame log cabin that could have been right at home if it was plopped down in Montana or Texas. The bar was surrounded by wood paneled walls and the place oozed charm. Everyone I spoke to was excited about my trip and gave advice about breweries I should try. I felt confident that this was a warmer welcome to Oregon than I would have gotten from family.

Just a short thirty-minute drive after a relaxing visit with the good folks in Sisters the breweries in Bend, Oregon came into view. I started with one of the big boys, Deschutes, and as expected they had it dialed in. It was a big, beautiful location which had that corporate feel of a brewery that had made it to the big leagues. The beer was consistently drinkable, and I was happy to be there. All breweries (as far as I know) have the same humble beginnings in someone's home. When a beer drinker becomes a home brewer you never know what might happen. Scaling one to this size is an interesting process, one that I've had the privilege of seeing firsthand.

Back in 1995, we had one of the sweetest girls ever working in our kitchen's pantry. She was such a nice person it seemed a little off brand when she kept complaining about her husband and his friend. No matter what she said or did they would not stop talking about starting a brewery. I had no idea what to say to her, so I just kept smiling and sympathizing. Men right...

They kept going, those men, and they just happens to

be the co-founders of Stone Brewing, one of the biggest brewers in the world and a main component of the brewery expansion in the San Diego area. Those first years were amazing. I was invited to all the parties and came out with swag galore as a way of promoting their brand. Those were some exciting times. A few years later I was lucky if I could just get in the lottery for a ticket to an anniversary party! It just goes to show you, we never know what amazing things can happen.

Leaving Deschutes for something a little grittier I headed out to find some funk with the likes of Crux fermentation and Bone Yard Brewing. Both housed amazing beers within a "I brewed this in my garage" kind of feel. At Crux, I bought a bottle of stout called "Tough Love." Little did I know that was exactly what was in store for me further down the road.

Had I not been wandering around both states with an open mind and a sense of adventure I may have missed some of these powerhouses but according to many of the beer guzzling dudes I've run into since, apparently, I was on the beer-oriented road trip of a lifetime! My buddy Steven who was running the tap room back at Societie Brewing in San Diego had been keeping up with my blog. He kept messaging me, thanking me for wearing their sweatshirt at all these places and saying how jealous he was. And I hadn't even been to Portland yet!

Somewhere in Bend I laid my head down for the night, content as I could be. As I gassed up for the next day, I noticed a sign on the front of the station that said, "growler fills inside." This was news to me. Filling a growler was a never-ending battle in California due to the constantly changing laws. Here, you just had to make a stop for gas.

Curiosity (of course) got the best of me, so I gingerly walked toward the growler fill station and suspiciously asked if they allowed tasters. It seemed impossible that someone would offer you a drink having no doubt that you'd be getting on the road, right? The guy behind the counter just asked what I wanted to try! So, with a full tank of gas and a full growler of black cherry stout, I was back on the road.

CHAPTER 24: KEEP PORTLAND WEIRD

To have a grand homecoming maybe you have to have provided a grand home in the first place.

During a summer rain shower I stood in a line that wound five layers deep outside Voodoo Doughnuts for forty-five minutes without an umbrella. That's just one of those things you have to do while in Portland. Menus had been passed about as we waited, which was really just a waste of time because whatever you thought you wanted went right out the window when you finally set foot inside. This has to be one of the funkiest doughnut shops in the world. Imagine all the food at the county fair on top of or stuffed into a doughnut...but on crack. As you snake around the secondary line once through the entrance of the store you get your first glimpse inside the glass walls of the round swirling doughnut showcase. Maybe there were about forty or more assorted types to choose from. I'm not even sure it was legal for some of those toppings to be on food. I was so frazzled by the time it was my turn to order I just pointed to four that looked the best in the moment, paid the fifteen bucks, took my box, and left.

Across the street, as my car sat facing the gigantic Keep Portland Weird mural, I sat facing off Voodoo himself. I propped open the lid of the pink box and stared at what I had in front of me. Feeling nothing like the girl staring down the ice cream section in the grocery, I dug in. This was an experiment and I had to just go for it. It didn't take long for the spell to be broken. There was no magic in these doughnuts for me, the hype was all in the boldness and multitude of the combinations. It was like plucking the cutest thing out of a display and wondering why it's not that great when you get it home. Merchandising.

Unable to get past a second bite of any, I chucked the box in the trash and drank a full bottle of water in one long lingering gulp. I did feel like I'd contributed to keeping Portland weird though. Close at hand, an outdoor market was in progress and the rain had slacked just enough for me to stop in and take a peek. Colorful tents of goods and the aroma of street food…what's not to love.

Next stop was the Pearl District where I got another chance to visit a Deschutes Brewery. This location offered an entirely different feel, less corporate, more of a neighborhood hangout vibe, with two or more seating areas. I choose a seat at the bar and after a delightful lunch accompanied by a sampler of beers walked a few blocks to Powell's Books, another must see in this quaint city. Powell's takes over an entire block and is the largest independent seller of both new and used books. You can get lost in there but the newly found minimalist in me just browsed for a bit.

Just a few blocks down the way were Rouge and 10 Barrel breweries, neighbors sitting closely located to one another. Each boisterously filled with an entertaining crowd on that Saturday night. I took the steps to the upper patio at 10 Barrel and looked out over the street while sipping one of their fresh draft selections. I wondered if I'd ever get used to this feeling.

From there I snagged another Airbnb and just enjoyed the rest of the evening. Portland was just two hours from my son's place. I'd be there by tomorrow which just happened to be Easter day. Two full years since my work exodus had begun. Was that destiny? It certainly felt like it.

Portland definitely projects a certain vibe, and I had dug that funkiness for sure. They have a wonderful metro system. I met a man riding it who said he hadn't taken his car out of the garage in seven months! I still had to hop back in mine though and moving north the natural beauty of the scenery along the coast was much more rugged, but the landscape was far greener than what I was used to. It was a mesmerizing drive with snow-capped mountains, lava beds, rivers and waterfalls sitting right alongside the road. Luckily, I hadn't run headfirst into any deer!

Things had begun to feel more natural in many ways. Slowly it felt I was living instead of rushing around just to exist. And it wasn't just about having the time or the freedom, there was something more, something deeper happening, similar to being awakened from a dream state and suddenly finding out what's real. Life rather than stuff had begun to feel more tangible. The churn of that grind to keep the accumulation moving had kept me trapped deep in the facade. It felt very much like I'd been lied to all along. Portland's weirdness had been refreshing.

The three weeks without a home during a two-thousand-mile road trip had suited me just fine. I'd spent less than I would have on a vacation and had done whatever I wanted to without worry or question. Overall, it was a colossal success, and I still had no plan. It seemed like I should be scrambling to find housing, but it was almost an afterthought. A burdenless afterthought. There were times when I thought living in a small RV on the road might have been the way to go. I could picture myself at a campsite with my feet in a stream somewhere, anywhere. But it was another one of those things that were just not meant to be, and I was fully into allowing things to happen as they may. Certainly, there must just be times when this is necessary because had I been able to foresee what was in store for me I wouldn't have agreed to any of it willingly, even though it all became exactly what I needed most.

The next morning, I crossed into Washington state and when I arrived at Williams place, he had only a few minutes to spare for me. Not wanting to cramp his style I took a room at the Red Lion down the street from his apartment. After a hot shower and a meal, I collapsed onto the bed and burst into tears. I was there. Where I had intended to be and somehow I felt far more lost than I had at any point during those past two years. A flood of emotional weariness washed over me, exhausting my energy. Maybe it was the loss of total freedom. Maybe this was where I needed to be. Or perhaps it was just setting the tone for the energy yet to come. I hadn't expected there to be fanfare, or an enthusiastic greeting on my arrival. I knew the relationship with my son was one in progress, but I had hoped to feel welcome rather than just there. I didn't feel unwelcome. It was more of a neutral, take-it-or-leave-it welcome. At least I knew better than to say anything at that time. It would be a long while until I would understand why I didn't deserve the warm welcome I longed for. There was absolutely no one to blame but my own poor parenting.

A few disheartening days later, I moved my life over to an Airbnb located in the gorgeous Gig Harbor area where we'd vacationed. I reached out to the lovely Mindy, who I had rented the room from during my month long stay in Keith's neighborhood. It was so nice to have some company who wanted to show me around and was fun having as a guide. We took in some great meals, a few movies, the zoo and did a bit of shopping. And I still could not wrap my head around finding a place to call home. The answer came when my friend Emma called me from San Diego. She wanted to know if I'd fly to Charleston, South Carolina and help her mom do what I had just done, sell everything and move. I was in! I'd stayed with them in Charleston several times and I knew this would be a grand adventure, apparently just what I had been waiting for!

I hung around enjoying more of Gig Harbor while Emma and her mom Jean were working out the details. After William and I's last stay in Gig, I expected to see deer each morning as I rose, but not a one showed up. Maybe it was William who had summoned them, it wouldn't have been the first time.

During one of our more adventurous summers when he was around twelve we thought a white-water rafting trip might be fun. We chose to head north so we could tour the state's capital too, and with the assistance of someone from work who doubled as a travel agent, the arrangements were made. The morning as we drove to the airport it was as still as it was early when something shot out from the side of the road and ran right in front of our car. I remember thinking, ahh hell no, a black cat, that's not a good sign. William told me I said something like "William, did you see that? What the hell was that? Was that a freaking black cat?".

The cat turned out to be a harbinger of things to come. It started with an issue with our flight that sent us across the tarmac and onto a puddle jumper rather than a larger jet. We had a few surprises at the state capital but the first day of rafting went rather well. As we shoved off the dock to launch our exploit down the river, our guide paddled lazily and ran through our instructions. Do this if this happens, that if that happens, but when nothing was said about what to if you fell out, I asked. Our guide laughed and told us that never happens. "Yeah, well what if it does" was my next question. She just didn't sound ready enough with an answer for that question, but I let it go and off we went.

With water splashing on us, around us and into the boat we either paddled hard on the straight aways or leaned in when instructed. Otherwise, we just floated peacefully out in the middle of nowhere with a half dozen strangers. The big rubber raft gently drifted to the edge as we hopped into the cool water to pull it ashore for a lunch break. Our guide Gina emptied her pack tossing each of us fresh sandwiches, drinks and snack baggies of "GORP" which literally meant good ole raisins and peanuts. And I don't know how this happened to me, being the adult in our party of two, but I hadn't read the fine print about the overnight camping trip. It made perfect sense but hadn't crossed my mind until Gina asked if we were excited about it. I guess I just thought we were doing two days of rafting and forgot about sleeping in between.

Looking over at William, I asked if he wanted to camp to which he frowned and shook his head. We'd been down that road before and it wasn't one we were going down voluntarily again so we were happy to hear that we had other options.

Back on the river we floated and jerked along, having a blast, and laughed as each rapid sprayed us in the face or soaked our clothes. The biggest rapids were measured as 3.5, the hardest level being an unrideable level 5, so this was wild enough to hold our attention and just outdoorsy enough to feel adventurous and sporty. After a full day of river water, a boatload of newly acquainted strangers, the scents of the woods and all the GORP we could handle, we were ready to rest.

Up the road in the direction Gina was pointing would be a B&B just a few miles away. Winding our way there we were chatting away about our day and all of a sudden, right in front of the car was this set of eyes. An actual deer in the headlights. Nothing spectacular or out of the ordinary for my son but I froze like the deer and slammed on the brakes. William really thought I was nuts because the deer was actually on the side of the road, we were just on a turn that made it look like it was right in front. Mom, always a source of entertainment.

Just as my heart stopped pounding, we pulled onto the gravel lot in front of the old house we'd already reserved for the night. What happened next sounds crazy, and had it not happened to both of us I may have thought I imagined the whole thing. After we checked in and made it to our room William asked what we were going to do next as he stretched out on his twin bed.

I was rolling my head around, kind of stretching, looking for a way to get comfortable. More and more I felt a creepy crawly tingling feeling around my throat. My son had turned to grab the chocolate off his pillow but as his gaze passed over my face, he asked what was wrong. By then my palms were dripping with sweat and I was rubbing the front of my neck with my hand. I didn't want to scare my son, but I was really not getting enough air. I couldn't breathe.

"Mom, are you alright?" William asked, now looking scared.

"WE HAVE TO GO!" I nearly shouted. William said I was really pale as we grabbed our stuff and practically ran down the stairs. The nice man who'd check us in saw us coming, nodded his head and held up a finger. He'd be right with us. I went outside for air, William motioned when the attendant was ready. Without asking a single thing he said he understood and was already processing a full refund.

"What the hell was that?" was the most I could get out. Obviously, this was not his first rodeo. The room we'd been given was known for occasionally getting some strange reactions from guests. As I described what I'd felt he looked down, slowly nodding his head. The room we were in had been the bedroom of a woman who'd owned the house back in the 1800's who apparently was last seen hung to death in the basement. William and I ran to the car. This place had scared the shit out of us, and we couldn't get to the next place soon enough. We are not fans of creepy.

There had been a series of days when I was in high school when I kept dreaming of tragic accidents. A plane crashing on take-off, a train derailment or a motorcycle accident, stuff like this. I would dream it; the next day I would learn that exact thing had happened. Creepy.

We tried our best to grab a few hours of sleep to be ready for day two, our final day of rafting. We had a great time sharing our ghostly story, riding the river like we knew what we were doing and just as we were all complimenting Gina on a job well done, we reached the very last rapid. The passage was very narrow, and we must have caught it at just the right angle needed because the boat tipped up at and laid William and I flat on our back into the water.

William popped right back up and one of the guys grabbed him, pulling him back in the raft within seconds. He remembers asking where his mom was and seeing my handprint pushing up on the bottom of the boat. Either side of that narrow passage the walls were filled with jagged and sharp rocks. All I could think about was where William was while remembering not to panic. I couldn't see him. In the darkness hardly anything but the bottom of the boat was visible. I knew I had to swim out from under the boat and came up yelling his name when not one, but two of the guys pulled my big ass out of the water. There was William, as happy to see me as I him. I looked at Gina. Smart ass comments about how no one ever falls out of the boat on the tip of my tongue.

We never went rafting again.

CHAPTER 25: CLEANSING IN THE GENTLE BREEZES OF THE SOUTH

Peace rises in the tides of new beginnings.

Boating, however, was something I was eager to repeat and especially in Charleston. Just a few days after our original call, a plane ticket arrived in my name. The beauty of boating there with friends is that the trip eventually turns into a bar crawl. San Diego has very few restaurants that have dock and dine options, but Charleston has rows of them. It's not unusual to dock one or two boats deep and then navigate your way across each of them to the dock which is just part of the fun!

After navigating the tide charts Jean and I walked down the lengthy dock behind her house to the boat. Situated on the intercoastal waterway she had to be sure of both high and low tide, or we could get stuck with no way back home. We thought we'd go have some fun and plan our time together. Even though Jean was much closer to my age, ours was still a rather new friendship. I figured if she'd raised a wonderful gal like Emma we'd have a great time over the next few weeks.

I'd arrived in Charleston the night before and it was everything I remembered it to be, which is so different from anywhere else. Downtown, with its purposeful lack of tall buildings, has that small town feel. The overall tranquility matches the pace of the horse drawn carriages which add to the charm for us tourists. A subdued feeling of peace comes with the slowness, yet a subtle hint of lingering darkness seems to fill the nooks and crannies, a reminder of the area's embattled history. Pale sky-blue paint adorns the ceilings of many an outdoor veranda to ward off the demons.

Years back when I first visited, I'd been excited to look around, so the ladies and I headed out to do some shopping. They said we'd be going to the "slave market" just as casually as asking someone to pass the salt. I absolutely knew they meant no harm by this, but it did catch me off guard. It reminds me of how we normalize the things we have grown up with. This reference, for those who weren't negatively affected, may be simply a part of history. For so many it's been a nightmare lived over hundreds of years and perpetuated by a kind of basic unawareness of the pain it represents.

The market is believed to be the last existing facility for that gruesome purpose in South Carolina. Beautiful Gullah women sit outside the entryway weaving gorgeous baskets of seagrass by hand every day. Inside we met some enchanting Black women selling spices and chatted with them at length. The spice mixes were the best we'd ever tried.

Sometimes I think we have to confront the conditioned beliefs behind the traditions within our culture because they become our version of normal making it easy to overlook their effects on society as a whole. I do believe we as a nation are doing far better with that now, something I am continually interested in learning more about. Jean and Emma were great examples who had it wired because they both were fully and kindly accepting of others, and it was a privilege for me to spend time with them.

As the sun rose the next day so did my friend Jean and she was raring to go. The steady calm of last evening's meal on the water along with the tranquil lull of the boat ride which provided a great night's sleep was already a thing of the past. It was time to enlist my old friends' Offer Up and Craigslist and start a staging area for the many tag sales (as they are called in the south) we were about to set up.

Sorting through someone else's collections from a life infused in the rich traditions of the south was an honor. With each pull of a drawer, cabinet, or closet door a new story would burble up from the past and continue on to be shared with others during our sales. I wondered if half the people who came by were shopping or just wanted to visit and when many of them came back week after week I had my answer.

From the start I found myself fully enamored with the trash cans, a whole new relationship for me! I had to monitor them diligently because while Jean was not a garage sale aficionado, she was a southern gentlewoman. She'd shriek with each half empty can of spray paint or rusty tin of tools I'd pull out of the bins, not wanting to be embarrassed by selling such horrid used things. But after the first sale when those rusty treasures became the most sought-after items she smiled, shook her head, and went to find more of the same.

The two-story house had closets in places I'd not thought to look, and each was stuffed with unique, cool, and vintage pieces. Some days we might hire a neighboring kid to help us drag them down to the basement level, some days we'd start out with the energy to do it ourselves. Some of the things I'd be attaching price tags to were swept aside mid-pricing for various family members to pick up. As the place thinned out and the dough rolled in I found Jean stashing the funds in a random canister in the kitchen; tucked inside was a slip of paper with a running tally and she was doing well. We were tired but happy and having a great time together. To break it up we'd hop on the boat or take a quick car trip to a nearby bar and restaurant. We were both thrilled when Emma came for a week to sort through her room and join in the adventures.

Near the end of my stay, I took a day trip to Savannah when Jean had other things to do, (although I secretly suspect she wanted a break from me). As I sashayed my way down the cobblestone streets aside the waterway, occasionally gazing idly in the shops or stopping by a kiosk I felt very southern myself. Like every cool city there was a tour to be taken and fortunately a bar near the boarding zone. With time to spare I plopped down on a barstool right in front of a sign as bright as the sun proclaiming, "Beers we do not carry" which listed the most commercially common beers. It was like they knew I was coming!

The southern gentleman tending there, and I had a great conversation about our love for craft beer and my recent road trip. I thought we were simpatico, but when he set my glass in front of me I noticed it was a plastic to-go cup while everyone else had nice frosty glasses. I looked to see if mine read *get the hell out of here* anywhere on the cup. The barkeep asked (with a laugh) if I was going on the tour. He'd spotted the sticker on my shirt and assumed

I'd want to take my beer to go! Could this get any better? I had no idea Savannah was like Vegas and New Orleans where alcohol can be consumed everywhere but it was sure awesome to learn. The tour was one of the better ones. I topped off the day sitting along the impressive Savannah River for a spell before starting back towards Charleston. Full and fully charmed by the South all over again.

Even though Jean and I had been working hard for a month and a half the time still flew. Transitions like this churn up a lot of emotions and while we both wanted the next chapters of our respective lives to begin we were truly sad to see this period end. We'd accomplished so much together. We'd emptied an entire house, found some great tenants to rent it, sold the boat and a pair of jet skis; and made a lot of new friends along the way. The crazy and amazing family across the street who had been such great company the entire time were the people moving in!

My flight headed off to the Pacific Northwest with a grateful but nostalgic passenger in tow. A finale to my grand adventure, an exclamation point on my transition to a new life ahead, and once again, there I sat, with no plan in place.

CHAPTER 26: STILL DISLODGED AFTER ALL THIS TIME

The calm before the storm is not just a saying.

As the light bounced off the lake and the rays fell over my Adirondack chair, I realized I'd been lounging around in other people's spaces for over three months. I was back in Gig Harbor but had just booked a stay in the Capitol Hill neighborhood of Seattle because I was expecting my first visitor. Gerard wanted to watch the fireworks on the 4th of July over Lake Union. We lucked out when our Airbnb sat across the street from a quaint kitschy Seattle-esq restaurant and bar. Couldn't be easier, or so I thought. Sometimes being too close offers a false sense of security.

We loved the fireworks and were having the best time. Before I fell off my bar stool, I took the road (which was somewhat spinning in front of my eyes) home and crossed the street to get some sleep. Gerard - not so much.

Which meant my much-anticipated sleep was interrupted by a series of progressively drunken phone calls! Gerard's wrong turn left him lost and sleepless in Seattle and his last call informed me he'd been kidnapped by the Russians. Funny now, not at all funny at the time.

When he finally found his way back to sleep it off, I took the opportunity to shop for a mattress, even though there was no place for it to go. That day kicked off a whirlwind of progress. I found an apartment, signed a year's lease signed, had the mattress delivered, and picked up the stuff that had been shipped from California and was being stored at my son's house. Gerard was helping all along the way.

So, after a sad trip of dropping Gerard at Sea-Tac, I went home for the first time in months. The climax of a transition I hadn't seen coming. It felt awkward and strange. The emotions were creeping back in, setting me adrift in thought. As I've mentioned, life has swept me along in ways for my own good so many times, but most of the time we don't really get to see that until much later, if at all.

My hope was for some much-needed time with my son, but I had to step cautiously there. This wasn't about me; this was about him. The friend I'd met on my month-long stay, became my saving grace in those months, as I learned my way around the Puget Sound area. God does place the exact right people in your life as needed, even if at times, only for a while.

It hadn't been my intention to become a renter at that time because I was still stuck on the belief that owning property was necessary. I started a search to see what the area had to offer, and I met a really great husband-and-wife pair of realtors. Suddenly, there were too many options and none of them seemed just right.

Buying a house would either eat up most of my cash or send me right back to work. Buying a condo meant taking on monthly HOA fees. Flipping a house would be all new to me. We diligently looked at everything. At one point, I even kicked around the idea of starting a staging business. I printed up some cards, calling it Renew & Prosper, and spoke to a few potential clients including another realtor.

But nothing was really sticking. The change in climate and scenery was a good one and more time spent with William was a blessing. Everything around was so green and for the first time I knew all four seasons. My very first Christmas there was white. I had a little balcony in my little apartment complex which had a wonderful view.

Over the next eight months the lovely pair of realtors must have shown me eighty different options, sometimes tagging in other realtors to change our luck. I fell in love with one I spotted a for sale sign on and seriously thought it was the one. It was a 60's style custom home with dynamic, sweeping views. We'd even negotiated a deal where the owner would carry part of the purchase price, but I still couldn't pull the trigger. This was such an amazing opportunity that I pleaded with friends to become investors to see if that would push me along, but it was again one of those things not meant to be. For some reason I was stuck on another location, a condo complex that had caught my eye for its proximity to the water and incredible pricing. We'd placed three offers so far and not one had been accepted...again, not meant to be. Or at least not then.

Finally, we were almost ready to go on the flip of a hundred-year-old home and the team had brought along a contractor to assess the renovation. Judson ended up being the only keeper in this crew. He pulled me aside to discuss how much work the house really needed, and while he didn't want to interfere he did mention he had a realtor friend. At this point I am positive the couple I'd been working with were more than happy to see me go!

And, as there are no coincidences, Judson's friend happened to be the very same realtor I'd talked with about doing some staging! What are the chances? So, I met up with Dallas the next day and he was just what I needed to help me reign in my choices rather than indulging my confusion. This ended up being the key to unlocking my success as well opening the door to my next big and unbelievable phase of this journey.

When I told Dallas about my condo obsession he agreed to keep a look out and sure enough, after showing me only two other properties, another unit became available. The price had already increased by 20 thousand from the first offer I'd placed but Dallas was a man on point. The minute I directed him to the listing he met me there within the hour and told me to make a full price offer if I was serious about buying. The next day we had a deal. Eight months and 20 thousand more later, the last offer I made was in the same building as the first one and I was again a property owner. After all that I thought I'd find a calm sense of relief. But instead, this is where everything began to get really, really fucking crazy.

Whether a convergence of energy or a sudden trip and fall down a vortex of cosmic madness, my life would never, ever, ever again be the same. Just like what happened in the hanging hotel, I wouldn't believe any of it possible and I certainly wouldn't have chosen it.

As the condo went into escrow a studio apartment opened up in my building. When I first rented the one bedroom I was put on a list for a studio, so it was offered to me first. Immediately after that I got the very first (and only) call for dog walking services on the posting I listed months back in the building. And a day or so later I got a call from Tiffany who was beginning certification courses for life coaching. Her first module was going to be held in Seattle, and since she could invite a friend, she asked me.

It was a lot at once to seem random then, and I am now certain they were predestined. I may have even asked for all this. Right between the time I first started working with Dallas and we made the offer on the condo I had been sitting outside the café in my mixed-use apartment building. I was enjoying an iced coffee and thinking how great life was. I'd settled in here, felt comfortable and was moving forward once again. I'd still been doing my inner work, talking to Sean via phone and I was feeling so solid I said something like, God I feel ready for whatever you've got for me.

So, first, don't do that. Don't try this at home kids. Because God proceeded to rain down with a force so significant I thought I had actually lost my entire mind. They say we are only given what we can truly manage, but apparently we can be very unaware of exactly how much we can take. I was about to find out.

The condo was just a few minutes away from a gorgeous three-mile walking trail I was already very familiar with. I was picturing what life would be like living there. Yet, as Dallas and I sat in the condo waiting for the inspector to do his thing, it hit me, I didn't want to live there. I had this overwhelming feeling that if I was to move in, I'd become stagnant and die there. This condo may have been mine, but it wasn't for me.

Trying to get a grip, I walked out onto the balcony which overlooked a beautiful area covered in trees, a mini forest of sorts. Even the smell of the water was calming. But something didn't feel right. I'd already seen the studio that had come available in my building and loved it.

 Sheepishly I glanced at Dallas and told him what I was thinking. Let me just say this about Dallas, he doesn't care! He's all about getting it done. With a grin he opened his laptop and said, "Great, let's get it listed on Craigslist for rent then, I'll shoot you the photos right now!" And for some reason, even though I had been besieged with choice this one was easy. I placed the listing that night.

Within a day's time I knew in my gut I'd found my first tenant, which turned out to be true. Brittany had shown up the day escrow closed and said she was 99% she would take it. She just had to show the photos to her husband first. On the way out the door, she turned and asked me not to rent it out from under her saying that had just happened. I smiled. I did have a backup plan, someone meeting me there next, but we agreed it was hers if she wanted it.

Feeling happy for Brittany and I but a bit bad for the guy waiting, I walked out to greet him. I kept repeating his name to myself so I could at least appear to be professional while breaking the bad news. But as I saw a young man walking toward me my mind went completely blank. The strangest feeling came over me.

I have never reacted to anyone like this before. After our awkward meeting without the use of our names we both nodded and looked confused. This guy was overly familiar, (and I know how strange this sounds) he felt like everyone. I'd never met him before. I pointed to the door of the building trying to direct him as I diverted myself to the car with the intention of collecting (myself) some things for the condo.

There were two boxes of light fixtures in my arms as I turned...only to run straight into the guy. Without a word, as if it was the most natural thing to do, he took them out of my hands. Normally I would have been shaken but this weird sense of calm fell over me.

As he looked around inside I told him I was certain I'd found my tenant and instead of leaving he asked if I'd mind if he put the light fixtures up for me. He said he didn't care that it was rented, he just wanted to help me. There I stood, looking at this man, a stranger who felt like family, who I wished I could help, who was now offering to help me.

He grinned at me and said he was an electrician. Now what were the odds that the one and only thing I wanted to change out in this place were light fixtures and he would be an electrician. You can't make this stuff up. Had it not been for Brittany's last words he would have had himself a condo.

We talked long enough for me to learn that his name was Rusty. I said I had promised my new contractor friend Judson any work that needed to be done, and he asked me to let him know if anything changed. I told him of course, with a wave, put on my seat belt, shoved the car in reverse and quickly headed away from the building. This was the most unusual meeting of my lifetime, and I was not looking back.

The next day, scrolling through texts, I came across his. I knew I should text him to confirm the unit had been taken but being the confused and shaken woman I was in that moment, I deleted all evidence of him from my phone like any good coward would, thinking that was that.

A few days later, under a bright orange umbrella on a patio table that housed both my laptop and latte, I began to write. I had been keeping a journal thinking it may one day help others in the form of a book or a blog, or maybe I was just doing my own processing. Whatever it was, it was happening at the very same café I'd made the proclamation to God a short while before. A friend and I had been exchanging some texts, but I was surprised to see "Hi, cutie!", my friend would not say that. It was from an unsaved number.

I had to laugh. My logical brain knew it had been meant for another number, so I replied to let him know. All of a sudden I found myself in a wild text exchange. All I could do was laugh. It didn't stop, the messages ranged from outrageous, to shy, to funny, getting more and more hilarious with no end in sight. I'd been transported to a comedy club, and he'd finally found his audience. Even after I said goodbye and stopped replying, a few more popped up like those last stragglers at the tail end of a Fourth of July fireworks extravaganza.

I walked the short way home, grinning ear to ear and feeling like a kid. I re-read those texts several times laughing louder with each; and finally, around midnight, once again the whole thing was deleted. I refused to believe someone so young had actually been flirting with me but went to bed with a smile none-the-less.

And so, it began...

To be very clear I have no interest in turning this into either a romance novel or a work of science fiction, however, this shit is gonna get fucking crazy for a while. In the telling of my story, which is one of change, I can't leave this out. Not only because it's so unbelievable but also because nothing in my life has influenced more profound change so quickly.

The next days were so non-stop I thought I'd put all that silliness behind me. From moving apartments, celebrating William's birthday, attending life coach training, my new dog-walking gig, hanging out till 2 am at a bar with my new client and going to lunch with new coaching friends, I had been busy. Even though the coach training consisted of three long 10-hour days, that were held in an unimpressive hotel meeting room I liked the course and the group so much I signed up to complete my studies. I even found time to buy a new sofa.

Once the move was finished and that bad boy with its cool leather and dual recliners was in place, I was ready for a break. Most of the things I'd been buying, other than the bed, had been from offer up. I was not going back into consumerism, but when I had a chance to replace the garage sale sofa I'd been using with a great deal from Costco, I went for it.

The stage was set for a relaxing movie night at home when my phone signaled an incoming text. Nope. I wanted to ignore it but as a parent you really can't. And there it was, a message from an unsaved number and whoever it was wanted to know if I wanted to get drinks. I sighed and set the phone down.

I remember a day in Yosemite when my family and I hiked to the top of a huge rock formation. There was this guard rail. It guess it there to protect people from falling down what looked like a very steep drop. The rail was about five feet wide. Several feet were left open and unprotected on both sides. Anyone could have walked around and easily fallen right off the edge of that cliff.

At the time we were there, a small boy was holding onto the side post, running around it in circles. With each pass he was putting himself on the outside of the railing. My palms sweat thinking about it and that was years ago.

My palms were sweating just as badly as I sat on that new couch looking at my phone. Was I getting too close to the edge? It made no sense why I was so unnerved.

Just to be sure, I sent a text and asked who it was. "Rusty", he said, "you remember me, right?".

I closed my eyes.

CHAPTER 27: THE SOUL HAS A PLAN

When we are bound to face our darkest places keeping an open mind is the only option.

I thought about the moment when I said I was ready for whatever came next. It was right out loud. And so many changes had happened right away after that; wasn't that enough. From somewhere deep within I knew there was something that was being ushered in with this guy.

My reaction to this man was what bothered me the most. I've been friends with all types of people, and I think being confused most of my life helped me tune into people based on energy more than appearance. I knew the hesitation I felt about Rusty wasn't because of his age or how he looked. Eventually I'd recognize this was a deeper recognition of the soul, and maybe that was the issue, that unknown factor. Those connections, the ones that are meant to shake you to your core, bring along with them apprehension. Like a little warning sign from the soul.

I picked the phone back up and asked why he would want to have drinks with me. He said why not? He must have felt my hesitation because he called me. Who calls people anymore? He was at a grocery store right around the corner from my apartment. I could walk there, what were the odds. So, I agreed to meet him there.

I have this little book called -a line a day- that a friend gave me so I could keep notes from each day. This just happened to be the birthday of my school buddy, Jeff Brown. And this would not be the last time when dates held meaning when it came to Rusty.

I was stalling so much that Rusty called me again just as I walked into the store. He was coming around the corner out of an aisle and when I saw him I was floored. The grin on his face was enormous, and he would greet me with that grin each time we met in the future. The next thing I knew we were walking around that store like we were having the time of our lives. Like small children who had found their long-lost best friends. It felt absolutely magical. Weird but magical.

I know how ridiculous this sounds. And thinking about it later I would feel ridiculous myself, but not in that moment. I can still feel that energy. I am certain this was predestined and meant to happen just as it did.

Giggling like kids, we checked out and stood right outside the front entryway. I looked at him closely. I felt absolutely safe with him, so I invited him to my place. There we sat on the couch right next to each other, arm's touching. We talked all night long. He wanted to see photos, like we were friends catching up after years apart. He let out a laugh when he came to the one of me with Shamu, pointed to the TV where the movie Black Fish was on in the background. The second coincidence of the night but only the tip of the iceberg of what was to come.

I couldn't help noticing what a beautiful voice he seemed to have, and when I asked what his last name was I was overcome with a rush of feelings. His name sounded perfect, like I'd been waiting to hear it my entire life. It felt like I had returned to a place I'd longed to be. There was nothing to compare this to, no reference point. This was the most unusual I'd felt about anyone in my lifetime.

Rusty asked how old I was and then called me a liar when I told him fifty-six. He said there was no way, and as if he could just change it he declared that we were both thirty-five. It seemed like there was an incredible pull between us. He laughed and said, "imagine what it would be like if we'd met when we were both in our prime".

Maybe he was able to sense what this was far before I could or maybe he was just drunk but either way he didn't want to leave. By 4:30 I told him I needed to get some sleep, even though I had nothing to do the next day. He just moved his car and parked right under my balcony, calling me to talk for another hour.

Rusty was just twenty-eight. I was twice his age, which makes us twenty-eight years apart. Our birthdays are twenty-eight days apart. Later, when I looked up the spiritual meaning of the number 28, it said that an old phase of your life is ending, and you are about to start a new journey that will be tremendously spiritual. I wish I'd known to look that up a bit sooner.

There are some people that are meant to catch our attention so thoroughly, in ways we can't miss because they are here to bring something to our lives. I've had this happen with other people, just not like this. I believe that only once in a lifetime do we encounter what I was about to experience.

I was at least somewhat prepared. I'd been on this path for a while now and the coach training worked with levels of energy. Mine were raging all over the place. Obviously, I was right where I needed to be because I was going to need all the help I could get.

Within that week Rusty and I saw each other two more times and texted often. One night we were talking about doing something together for our birthdays. He stopped and said, almost to himself, they will just have to get over it, as if thinking of what people would think if we did.

There were moments – let's say brief moments - when maybe we both thought about being more than friends. Everything is energy, and the energy around me had become completely different in ways I couldn't wrap my head around.

I certainly didn't understand why it seemed like his energy was around me almost all of the time. It felt to me as if Rusty no longer left my side. I'd turn away from the kitchen sink and feel like I was running into him. His face would appear in front me out of nowhere. There was no longer stillness, there was a current that seemed to be buzzing, all the time. In a new level of bizarre, I was having both visions and dreams seeing ethereal versions of the two of us in an embrace, completely drenched in a blue-violet light. What the hell was this? My tiny studio was becoming far too small for the two of us.

Emotionally I bounced from calm serenity to an energetic onslaught of paranoia without knowing why. It felt as if I'd stepped out of reality and into another world. A world that took my emotions and threw them into a blender which was set on high. Thank the Lord I'd done the work to be fine by myself, this would have been unbearable without that inner peace. Still, nothing helped me understand why my heart was flopping around like a fish out of water, gasping for breath.

My heart, as it turns out, was the first to be tasked with

the hugest of lessons. I had this strange feeling to keep an eye out for Rusty while running errands one day. It was almost like a warning. And there he was, arm in arm with a girl his own age at Trader Joe, and he was definitely avoiding me.

My heart sank. Unfuckingbelievably, it sank. Why, why, why would I care at all? In a daze I made my way through the store and away from the parking lot before I stopped and just sat in my car feeling both stupid and crushed. Emotions came flying at me in a rush of energy that could have stopped a train on its tracks. This was not your normal everyday involvement. I sat there, feeling a profound sense of loss like nothing before. If I had been younger, or less experienced with relationships, I think I wouldn't have felt so insane about all this. It just seemed like I should know better, but the intensity of this was beyond my brain; it was directly affecting my heart right down to my soul.

Flight or fight kicked in, and I was ready to run, and run fast. My old tendencies of having one foot out the door resurfacing. I didn't tell him I'd seen him, but I did tell him didn't want to see him anymore. He didn't understand, and kept saying we were just friends, why couldn't we stay friends. He was right, why couldn't we be friends.

I wasn't about to share my internal chaos with him. I didn't dare say because it felt like so much more because

I didn't know how to describe it. I just said I couldn't get enough emotional separation from him which was absolutely the truth. And then he said he should get back with his ex anyway and I have no idea what that had to do with any of it.

The profound feelings of loss returned with a vengeance. For three days straight, I cried, and nothing helped. I could not explain it and I could not stop crying. Finally, Tiffany said to just call him because there was no reason to not just be friends if it was this bad. She was right. I felt so insane. Of course, that made more sense than living in an unexplainable pain. He was happy to hear from me.

 The biggest thing I did wrong in all of this was expecting it to be normal. I kept trying to align it with past friendships, because that's what the logical mind does, tries to make sense of things. I should have known it would only continue to be different, very different.

The next thing that came up was physical. As I was driving I began to feel a really strange feeling in the center of my chest. Like a warm bubbly feeling which kept getting more intense until I wondered if I would have to pull the car over. It wasn't scary, like something was wrong with my health, it felt more joyous and apparently this area is the heart chakra. This continued regularly for close to two years and I couldn't pinpoint any specific thought or feeling that would have caused it but I hadn't felt it until I met Rusty. Everything that had to do with Rusty was amplified by a million.

When my dog walking client, Jackie and her husband were in the process of flipping a house, they needed an electrician, so I put them in touch with Rusty. When I checked in with her she told me they'd had to fire him because he had doubled his estimate midway through the job. I totally lost my shit. Just like the reaction to seeing him at Trader Joes, it came out of nowhere. Logically, I can't explain why I was so extremely outraged by what he'd done. This was about five weeks after we met yet I was calling him up and getting in his ass like he was responsible to me. Clearly, I needed some help.

CHAPTER 28: SEEKING TO EXPLAIN THE UNEXPECTED

The doors we least want to open hold all the value.

In coach training I'd struck up some decent conversations with my classmates during our down time. I wasn't sure who to talk to about the big emotional ball of energy I had become but decided to stick my toe in the water over lunch one day with a classmate named Jackson. After sharing some of the blow-by-blow highlights I told him it felt like I'd known Rusty before. Jackson leaned back on his chair contemplating what to say next. He knew a woman who was an energy healer specializing in past life situations. I just stared at him. And frowned. But then, in gratitude smiled, that's how desperate I had become.

In the beginning when you hop on the emotionally

charged rollercoaster that is a soul connection, you just want answers. You want to be able to continue to navigate your life and if you don't know what rabbit hole you've fallen down you just feel lost. Or at least I did, and I wanted answers badly. Things were clearly no longer black and white, so I made the call into this all-new grey area.

After the woman, Charlie, answered I only had time to ask her rates before she started speaking. She said my energy was so strong that I just had to let her tell me what she was getting. I fell silent. She knew my situation involved a man and said she'd never before felt a connection as strong as ours. Then she rapidly described vivid details of three past lives she believed we had together. In all three he'd left me tragically.

Normally I would not have thought much about what she had to say but in every one of these lives the people she described had traits of both Rusty and I.

Charlie then asked if I'd heard of soul mates to which I groaned out loud. "No, wait" she said (what could be worse than telling me this man is my freaking soul mate?). "Twin souls" she said...we had an eternal connection. There was nothing I wanted to hear less than that. Something inside of me still wanted to run even though it was starting to look like there was nowhere I could go.

The whole call took less than an hour and her fee was nearly nothing. I hung up, put my head down on the desk and wept. I had not wanted to feel like I was being choked to death in a hotel with my son as a witness, and I did not want to have an eternal twin soul. If I was struggling in less than two months, how was I going to manage eternity like this?

At least give me a place to start looking for some explanations. It turns out Google knew about twin souls. They are most often referred to as twin flames. And let me tell you, what I read was shit. My radar (hidden fear) had been pushing me to run and this made me think it was the right thing to do. Still, it was all there, in writing. Other people, and lots of them were having similar experiences. At least this helped me feel less insane.

I sank into the sofa, curled up in a ball and turned-on Netflix. I was mad. Mad at myself, mad at God, mad at the woman on the phone and mad at Rusty who's energy was relentlessly all around me. I was pissed that I'd agreed to open a door that was such a huge pain in the ass. And when I went to the next module of coach training, I learned I had been living in my head and not my heart. I was mad all over again.

The next time I saw Rusty I told him about the phone call. He looked confused and asked why I'd called her. I told him I just didn't understand what was going on between us. He scrunched up his face and said, "you know we have a connection, right?". I asked what made him say that "because I pay attention" he answered. So, I took a chance and told him about the past lives which he said sounded about right. All I could do was wonder if I'd somehow dropped into a parallel universe.

Later that week, there I was, standing in the strip mall parking lot near the grocery store where this all began, screaming at Rusty. We'd just had a very relaxing dinner. Being around him wasn't ever the problem, in fact the time we spent together was filled with an unusual peace. This was the first time we'd gone out anywhere since we met, and I did not want him to leave. Something inside me ignited an outburst fit for a two-year-old. This was the worst I'd ever acted around anyone, and for no reason at all. And it kept happening the next few times we went out. In a flash, it would be gone and we'd both stand there looking at each other wondering what happened. Rusty, unphased, would just smile and say he'd see me tomorrow.

I needed to do something about those outbursts, so I set up a call with Sean. I happily relaxed to the sound of his voice, following the stairway down into the darkness of my subconscious, which had proven just as easy to do by phone as in person. I didn't understand where I landed.

So far each visit had taken me on a trip down memory

lane, overflowing with childhood trauma and nothing else. This time it was startling to find myself in the 1800s standing atop a darkened cobblestone street somewhere in England. Next to me was someone I knew to be Rusty, in a totally different body. Long into nightfall, a chill in the dampened air had us huddled together under an arched walk-through enclosure.

I could feel that we were destitute. Bundled heavily in long, thick clothing we spoke in hushed tones, fearful of detection. It was up to me; he'd been saying with deep sadness. His eyes, filled with weariness urged me to stay but his voice was telling me to leave. He said I knew what I had to do. I needed to be the one to leave him. I had no conscious idea why it was dangerous for us to stay together but we both knew he would not leave me.

 The same pain arose in my body that devastated me for that the three-day separation I had caused. I saw myself stiffen, the tears blistering my cheeks in the harsh cold. Slowly I turned to my left and began to walk away from Rusty. Pausing, unable to look back, I could hear his coat tails as he began to move in the opposite direction. I was sobbing so hard Sean had us finish and out I came into today's world.

In this unfamiliar territory with Sean, it was hard to know what to say, but I had felt better somehow. It was not the release of past hidden pain from childhood we'd been used to, but it was a release. Somehow I'd taken a step in another direction when it came to how I could navigate myself with Rusty. The outbursts stopped immediately after that work with Sean. Whatever was triggered when he left had been healed by my act of leaving him in my own subconscious visit to our past.

It seemed important that I was the one to leave him. Were those triggering moments when I lost it and started screaming rooted in past life trauma? I thought back about the lives Charlie had described how Rusty had left me in each. Once he'd been shot and died, once he'd become distraught and mentally checked out, and once he'd been my dad and died when I was just five. He'd not chosen to, but he had left me stranded. Considering they stopped after doing that work, that was the only explanation that made much sense.

This connection, whatever it was, had me feeling deeply intwined with Rusty in ways I'd not known before and was hard pressed to explain.

Sean was familiar with the concept of twin souls. He asked me if I'd read anything by Edgar Cayce who he said had been one of the first to write about the topic. He said his mother had talked with him about Cayce's books often. This again was one of THOSE moments where I froze. This was the book my own mother had tried to get me to read at least fifty times when I was far too young to care. Again, I had to ask, what are the odds that Sean's mother talked about that, especially since he looked so much like my brother. I believe in God, a creator, a higher power and I've read the whole Bible, but I did feel pretty strongly that past lives are very possible.

After my call with Sean, I was able to relax into the friendship more until I started getting even more bombarded with what seemed like very specific messages. Suddenly, every song I heard applied to what was happening specifically in my life when it came to Rusty. I'm talking specifics pertinent to exact moments.

I'd been noticing repeating numbers for months but now it was all day long. I couldn't look at a clock without it being 11:11, 3:33, or 5:55. Patterns of repeating and mirrored numbers were everywhere in those days. Some people try and say this is the subconscious seeking this shit out, but this was happening in some very unusual ways.

Entering a small parking lot with four cars in a line, three of the four would have repeating numbers. And it happened all day long. As Rusty and I were driving together one day I noticed that a car turning into the driveway we were exiting had 1111 on its plates, which were right in my face. He said he hadn't noticed before. Then we drove right past Café 1111 and just looked at each other.

So, I told him that he stayed on my mind all the time and he nodded and said, "yeah, about 75% of the time right?" like it was normal.

So, once in a while when things got too strange I'd put in a call to Charlie who asked why I was so uncomfortable; she said Rusty was totally comfortable with me. I thought she was crazy, but I asked him about that too. "Oh my God, yes! I'm so comfortable with you!" was his answer. He said I felt like home to him and that he talked to me in ways he'd never been able to with anyone else before. He admitted that he told me everything. At times he'd call, and talk about his day, admitting he had no idea why he'd called me. So, it wasn't just me. When I saw him it felt like I could just melt right into him.

It was the times when he wasn't physically there, but still felt there that drove me nuts. But then, I'd see him again and I felt safer than ever being around this man. And so, it went...when we were away from each other my mind picked it apart and constantly scrambled to keep up with each strange new happening.

Rusty seemed fully fine and totally ok with whatever came up between us and unafraid of the craziness. In most ways we were total and complete opposites. Maybe Charlie was right when she called us two peas in a pod. Whatever this was, it started to feel that we were in it all together and that talk confirmed it. I felt closer to being myself when I was around Rusty. It was like he could see down past the bullshit of life, straight into my soul and accept everything about me. And I was feeling the same about him. It didn't matter that there was a huge age difference, or we weren't each other's type, we were there at that time, together as friends for a reason. When he left that night I heard him whisper "I love you" under his breath as I was shutting the door.

CHAPTER 29: NEVER-ENDING-WEIRDNESS

The truth of love is hidden behind pain.

Love. Missing in action from my childhood. Feverishly sought after in many relationships. Certain I'd cherished my son and sought to shower him with it. But now seen through the eyes of my own soul.

I was having lunch one day with a friend, telling her the latest when she said, "you know that's love right?" I'd been beating down every path I could find when it came to learning about twin souls and at that time there hadn't been much on the subject.

He and I did not seem like the stuff of mythology to me; not as referenced by Plato, being one until Zeus split us apart. But I still could not find one non-romanticized version of this journey. There was a definite premise that twin souls were on a mission and that involved physical union. While I did feel a deep sense of love in my heart at that time it didn't feel like we needed to be together romantically.

There were quite a few times when Rusty would spend the night sleeping next to me and say something silly while he hugged me. Occasionally he'd skip a workday and we'd spend the day goofing off like irresponsible children. Once he came over to hang a light and kept dropping stuff, saying he got butterflies around me. And sometimes he'd say he just wanted to make me happy.

The logical me thought it was all play, but my heart somehow knew it was more. And for a while I did fall down the rabbit hole and wonder if maybe we were destined to be together. And then something new would happen to scare me all over again.

I was at home enjoying the gentle breeze that flowed in through the balcony slider when I felt a low dull pain in my stomach. It was pretty intense but somehow did not feel like the pain was from my own body.

I Googled the area and found it was the location of the power chakra. What now, I thought. I lowered myself onto the bed and the phone rang, Rusty was asking me to lunch in the middle of his workday. It turned out he'd just gotten in a huge fight with his boss. A power struggle, you might say. It was his pain I'd felt. Energy is energy. At lunch I told him what had happened, and he agreed it was strange, I think he called me a weirdo!

And then one morning as I stared into the bathroom mirror this random thought drifted in about Rusty and ball caps, he never seemed to be without one. I didn't think any more about it until we met for lunch a bit later, him for the first time capless. His grin seemed to almost challenge me which I ignored like a pro. But then we met again, later on and still no ball cap. I wasn't going to give in and ask if he was projecting his thoughts or reading my mind. I didn't want to know.

And so, it would go. I walked a tightrope between what seriously seemed like Heaven and earth most of the time, not really knowing what to expect from one day to the next.

The clues were like breadcrumbs leading to an awakening too powerful to take in all at one time. Things that had not made sense in the past came to have answers. It started to make sense why my mom was so set on pushing me to read that Edgar Cayce book. There had been these two movies that had really haunted me. All the way back in the 80's the movie *Time After Time*, and a more recent one I'd seen the year before we met titled *In Your Eyes*, both hit me particularly hard for seemingly no reason. Now I could see they both resembled my current circumstances. There was also a period of many years where the smell of certain foods would randomly hit me.

The smell would be so strong it seemed like it was right under my nose. But those foods were never anywhere around me at those times. I had also been obsessed with a certain stone, not my birthstone, but the one that turned out to be Rusty's. My dad had even carried a few slivers in his wallet. Even my odd choice of soft drinks as a kid happened to be Rusty's drink of choice. Individual things held no special meaning alone, together they pointed in the same direction.

Whatever this was, the emotion around it mirrored a lot of the childhood pain that I needed to release. In that way we seemed to go back and forth like a tennis match, which triggered up a lot of stuff for each of us. Mine was showing me the way to healing my issues with love and food.

I was so driven to eat to have some type of interaction with my parents I was naturally a chubby kid. There was very much a feeling like I should not be disruptive. Even when I would run and try to play outside as a kid, if I fell and scraped or sprained something I was in trouble.

As I paid attention to the feelings triggered by Rusty and kept working with Sean, I was really starting to see how detrimental my childhood had been to my health. And then, to my own emotional state.

I was able to remember back to a time when both of my parents shamed me for being fat. It wasn't in hypnotherapy, it was on my own. Maybe it was a bad week for them, I'm not sure, but both seemed to tire of my interest in food at once. I can still picture my mother shouting at me, telling me to just go ahead and eat all the food in the house, so she wouldn't have to hear me ask for it again. I can see her walking away in disgust. Shortly after that, my dad looked at me with distain, and told me I was so big I was almost square.

I know now that I felt rejection, because food gave me a reason to be with them and they wanted to take that reason away. It caused a deep sense of shame. I was too little to be responsible for what I ate or, as a result, how I looked. I should not have been blamed.

For the young, sheltered, and shy girl who depended fully on the two people who rejected her, it was crushing. It broke more than my heart and spirit; it made me broken for all relationships to come. I recognize this as the marker when I shut down emotionally to protect myself. When those we depend on for safety create unsafe conditions a child's trust is broken, a sense of fear is instilled and even empathy gets pushed into the background to assemble some form of safety. We lose a part of ourselves because we don't know where we stand when we feel like we've lost our safety net.

So many moments and subtle messages left lasting scars indelibly inked upon my heart, shrinking my emotional understanding, keeping me hidden right out in the open. It took this connection to reach down to the bottom of my heart, unlocking it and breaking it wide open.

One day, Rusty looked up from a large bowl of Pho and told me that it was never-ending, whatever this was between us. I just shook my head. Another time he'd said how much better his life was since I'd been in it which caused me to smile. And at one point he said he knew I was a very important person in his life. I couldn't argue a single point he made. It was the steadiest limbo I'd ever been in and still hard to say exactly what it was at any given instance.

There would be times he'd outrageously flirt with me and times I'd flirt with him too. Once when I was hanging out with a mutual male friend he got frustrated and said that we'd be together if we were the same age. The times when I got frustrated and tried to ignore him I would see or hear his name a dozen times throughout the day.

One thing my dad used to say quite often was that he would teach me right from wrong, which I now see as more of a lesson in the beauty of contrast. Without dark we wouldn't have light. Acceptance of change: in things and people and concepts being different than expected is a tough and major lesson that doesn't come up in your average conversation. But an even crazier change was coming my way, which would freak me out entirely.

In 1973 on July 31st, (by the way, today as I'm writing is July 30th) a memorial service was held in downtown Seattle for Bruce Lee. That building eventually became a bar known as the Pine Box, which just happened to be where Jackson and I met for happy hour one afternoon.

We grabbed our bar stools and beers and as the conversation bounced between the dynamics of our varied lives it suddenly felt as if my entire body was on fire. Jackson noticed how red my face was, asked if I was ok. A second wave of heat caused me to jump off my stool and grab onto the chair back for stability. I felt very heavy and sat down again but felt as if I was being shoved into the background of my thoughts. Jackson's face had gone pale, and his eyes were wide. I sat staring intently into his eyes as words began pouring out of my mouth. Words that were not mine. This voice was entirely calm, and the words being spoken to Jackson were from a place of peace and serenity. I could hear them but not control them. And as quickly as it began it was done.

I felt myself gently drifting back to the forefront, exhausted. We decided to move off the bar stools and away from the bar. Just as Jackson started to tell me what had happened, I felt myself going off into the background again. Another voice came forth. Sterner and harsher in tone, this new message seemed more urgent, as if a warning in case the first message was ignored.

Jackson's face reddened. Visions of sand dunes passed by in front of my eyes and I faded a bit further back. I heard something about washing feet and humility. And again, as suddenly as it began it passed. I slumped and rested my head on my folded arms. Both Jackson and I were freaked out. According to google, twin souls can have increased spiritual and psychic abilities. Fuck this. FUCK THIS.

Unfortunately, it did not stop there. A short while later I drove past a car accident and got a feeling that I was being slashed right in half. It was very similar to when I'd felt the fight Rusty had with his boss. It was someone else's energy. Jackie had been with me and we stopped at a gas station to calm down and use the bathroom. I went in first to find all the lights flickered on and off the entire time I was there. Jackie said they stayed on the whole time for her. As if on que Rusty called and wanted to know what I was doing.

Another situation happened on the same freeway. I'd been chatting with Charlie and could not get her off the phone. I knew I would be late if I didn't get in the car, so I stuffed my earbuds in, grabbed my keys and headed to my car, her voice still chirping. Cruising along with a pair of motorcyclists up ahead I was presented with a challenging situation. It looked as if one of the bikers had taken off faster than the other. But the reality was, the one left behind was slowing down, and rapidly so. Stabbing my finger at the button to turn on my flashers, I yelled into the phone as I threw it and the earbuds to the floor. I decelerated to match the bike, praying that my 4-Runner had a better chance of being noticed in the center lane of the busy freeway than he did. Both of us slowed to a full stop. I glanced in the rear-view mirror, held my breath, and by the grace of God, no one was hurt. If I would have swerved around the biker, given the amount and speed of the traffic, I'm not sure what would have happened. It felt as if I'd been in the right place at the right time, which had happened because that phone call had delayed me. How much are you willing to open the door to peculiarity? Sometimes willingness has nothing to do with it.

CHAPTER 30: YOU BETTER BELIZE IT!

When you need a reset change the scenery.

Something had to break up the ever increasing crazy my life was becoming and fortunately, the perfect thing was on the horizon.

The trip to Israel had taken a bite out of my finances but I was happy I had chanced it. At the time I thought it may have been the very last opportunity I would get travel. But travel was still in the picture after all.

After months of intricate planning, followed by two planes, a shuttle, a puddle jumper, a taxi, a golf cart, and a boat, a group of eighteen descended on San Pedro, Belize, to celebrate our dear friend Nita turning the big Five-OH.

Two pristine white villas nestled in swaying palms adorned the private beach as we arrived, the only way possible, by boat. Conch shells splashed water gently into a large green glass bowl sink in the guest bath as we each freshened up and kayaks were stacked along the shore if the pool wasn't your cup of tea. We'd arrived in paradise. Nita is a planner and somehow she'd managed to find once in a lifetime accommodations that cost each of us less than a two-night stay in Sacramento.

Nita and I, along with two others, arrived a day early to set up, which went well into the night, as did the bottles of booze we'd picked up at the duty-free shop. With time for a celebratory lunch for a job well done, the next day we all hopped into the boat again with our resident villa keeper and boat captain and headed back into town. The spray of the water glistened on our joy filled, sun-soaked faces, and we were beyond happy.

A hut style bar complete with a thatched roof named The Office stood as gatekeeper of the dock. Here we were greeted by the whoops and hollers of the ever-friendly staff. The four of us walked along a dirt path amid the locals, who sauntered with the ease and grace of a people experiencing a far less stressful or finance centered lifestyle.

We strolled up to our chosen lunch venue. Impressive dark wood beams highlighted the open breezy beach front location, giving the impression that all of life was lived out of doors here in Belize. Whatever may have been lacking in first world polish was more than made up for in graceful simplicity and charm. Belize was a lifestyle where things happened when they happened and everyone seemed to be having a damn good time, all of the time. Gone was all pretense of American culture. Nothing was for show, everything instead for enjoyment. I walked along a greyish wooden dock, clearly the sun and wind had left it's mark. Palms waving toward the west with the tranquility of the sea visible as far as I could see.

That night the welcome party would great the rest of the guests where they'd each find their own custom gift bag filled with personalized flip flops, tank tops, wine, champagne and shot glasses. In our monthly mailers leading up to our excursion we'd found items like lip balm, water bottle holders, passport covers, watches set to the correct time, so many things, I can't remember them all. Nita had given us the gift of her birthday and we were swagged out.

The parties at our villas were the stuff of legends. The staff from The Office made it over most nights, as well as the tour guide from our sunset cruise and a few other locals we'd met along the way. I became of a combination of Stella getting her groove back and a girl gone wild on Spring break. I'd found my own alcohol induced groove.

Rusty texted urgently thinking I'd blocked him. Whatever made me crazy thinking we could not get in touch seemed to be happening to him too. Since we'd met I had somehow become a magnet for younger men. It was bizzare and it was happening there too. This was a once in a lifetime trip in some very unexpected ways for me.

After a very grand eight days, we all stumbled back to the airport, and I headed back to Seattle for the last three-day weekend of my coach training. As I was settling in for the last thirty hours of coursework, the door opened and in walked a new person. I stood, walked toward the young man, and gave him a big hug and warm welcome to our group. So strange, like I had known we'd become friends and exchange coaching in the future. Tom, it turned out, was having the exact same type of connection I was experiencing with Rusty. What are the odds.

Three days of work in a hotel banquet room is exhausting and coming off that trip like, I was toast. I have no idea how Rusty knew the exact moment I'd be free but he

reached out wanting to know if he could see me that night. Even that was an unusual visit. It was like he sensed how wild I had been and felt the need to be territorial.

Somehow that trip and the end of coach training marked a change of guard when it came to the energy and people in my life. Jackson, Charlie, and Jackie faded into the background along with quite a lot of craziness, much of which I have not mentioned. In came some new friends with very different energy.

In the building gym, I met Nana, who was from Africa

and had at one point been my next-door neighbor. She now lived three floors down. Shortly after, I met Anshu who was from Fiji, who had moved in next door when Nana had left. Two friends who had both been right next door all along, both much younger and both from other countries. I met Alexis at Whole Foods next door. All three of these young ladies became a wonderful part of my life.

Change only happened in bunches in my life. My condo tenants decided they needed more space and were not going to renew their lease. They said they'd be interested in leaving earlier if I could find a new tenant and I thought of Rusty. I told her I may know someone, and she asked if it had been the guy who'd seen it after her. I don't know why she remembered that. Of course, the next time I saw Rusty, as if he was in my mind with me, he started complaining about his living situation.

CHAPTER 31: THE NEXT PHASE OF THE JOURNEY

Shifts happen whether we like them or not.

I had been kind of happy with the status quo. I was building stronger boundaries, not just with the people in my life but also the weirdness. I continually worked on my relationship with William, and I wasn't fighting with food as much as I had before. Hypnotherapy was helping me unpack my emotional baggage, so I felt lighter all around, even though I hadn't lost any weight.

I was positive Rusty, and I were meant to be in each other's lives because we were both better when that was the case.

Things did not go well for either of us when we

fought. Arguments with him were like most things with him, very different. There was a weird feel to them, like they were not actually about either of us but about much deeper stuff. We were to trigger the past pain for healing. So neither of us stayed mad about anything at all. Things that may take me days or weeks to process with anyone else took hours with Rusty. There was almost an expectation between us that things would stay on a steady and peaceful course, no matter what came up.

Strolling along a downtown sidewalk in the evening with him, I might abruptly find myself in his arms as he reached over and bundled me up in a big hug out of nowhere. Casually chatting over beers on a wine barrel that served as a makeshift bar table, Rusty would lean in for a kiss, barely catching himself, and mumble that there was a natural attraction there. Wherever that attraction lived it was deeper than surface level. If not for it I'm positive neither of us would have given the other a second glance.

All of this contributed to my discomfort in renting to him. The constant splatter of emotional confusion had been causing me to face things I wouldn't have, otherwise. There was nothing keeping us in this thing except that we both wanted to be around each other. I feared that would change if he became my tenant. I think now, in the back of my mind, I must have had some sort of intuition of the changes this would bring. But I finally asked if he wanted the place and he jumped at the chance.

The blank slate that was my two-bedroom condo turned into a challenge for Rusty. He basically showed up empty handed with no means and apparently no friends or family willing to help fill the space. Off we went to turn one magnificent Saturday morning into a day of garage sale shopping. He went home to set up his new place and the next day I went in search of a new car stereo.

I spent the better part of the morning at Best Buy, waiting for installation, and on the phone with Rusty. As I strolled the isles, pushing buttons on the appliances, flipping the blu-rays upside down and feeling smallish under the huge, big screens, the surround sound nearly drowned out his voice through my earbuds. I don't know what was going on with him that day, but it seemed impossible to shake him. When I hung up he just kept texting me, which was not usual, but I didn't give it a lot of thought. Until a few days later.

Before I left the store, they showed me how to work the stereo, but I didn't listen to it again right away. When I did, damnit if I didn't see Rusty's name scrolling across the face. I turned it off and back on – still there. I skipped a day; it was still there. I was hoping it would go away but when Nana and I went out for happy hour she let out a shout when she saw it.

She thought it had to be because of an artist or the current DJ. I just looked at her. After our drinks she turned the stereo on, and it was still there. Rusty borrowed my car a few days later and asked how I'd done that. I'd bought a low-end stereo and there was nothing in the manual about programming a name on the display. This was something I could do something about. This was one part of the weirdness I could change. The next day I went in and had it exchanged. I told them that one just was not working for me. Problem solved.

And then I was introduced to Pam.

After being certified as a life coach I reached out to my photographer friend Remy who flew up to take some headshots for my website. It was grounding to be in the company of someone from home I'd known for so long. It was great to get back in touch and get reacquainted. I wanted this break.

We went out for drinks so we could catch up since a lot had changed since our visit in L.A.. I really wanted to avoid talking about all the crazy but when the topic of connections came up the door opened enough for Rusty to stroll right into the conversation. I had barely begun my tale of bizarreness when she smiled knowingly. As easily as if this was the next scheduled stop on the road map of my trip to the white padded cell, Remy recommended a woman her mom saw once in a while, who she thought may be able to help.

Before this began I didn't even read horoscopes. I do think people can be true to their astrological signs because I have all of the traits of my own, but I was not into any of that stuff much at all. Whatever this was with Rusty it was both the most intense and most peaceful experience of my life, all at once. I did want to know more so I called to set up a time to talk with Pam.

Rusty, in the meantime, was falling apart. His car was in the shop, he had no back up plan and had exhausted all his available favors. Which meant he wasn't going to work. Which meant he was unable to pay rent. He'd grown exceedingly quiet because he didn't know what to do. I had to either step in or kick him out. Together we figured out how he could get temporary transportation, and what he needed to say to his boss to get back in good graces and work again. Slowly, his life came back together.

Just as a little light began to shine onto Rusty it was time for my call with Pam, a woman well versed in the planetary, numerology, energy, and tarot. Once, in junior high I'd had a bad experience with a Ouija board, so I wasn't so excited about the tarot cards.

Pam was a lovely, authentic, and genuine woman. All she asked was my full name and birthdate and then began to tell me what she saw, which of course included a soul mate – but not just any soul mate, my one true soul mate. This person, she said, was the one I travel through every life with. That made me think of how he felt like everyone when we first met. She too, said it was pretty rare to be as connected in as many ways as she was seeing, and that we were...wait for it...a true power couple.

Sure...I thought, a couple of fools. The latest drama with him had worn me down a bit. I kind of wanted to walk off the set of this new movie and ease back into the one that had been cancelled.

CHAPTER 32: BREAKING

There is still room for choice even on the most guided of journeys.

I had a lot of trouble seeing us as any sort of a couple, let alone a power couple but when I shared it with Rusty it seemed to empower him. Or maybe he had come to believe that I'd always be around. This added complexity at a time when I wanted more agency, and I snapped under the pressure.

It began at a busy Starbucks where we met to talk about how to move forward. Rusty owed me some money for back rent and for helping him during his downtime and I wanted to know how he was going to work that out. He was not skilled at negotiating or maybe thought I was wrapped around his finger from Pam's proclamation. All I wanted was for it to be resolved. It did not go well. Rusty finally leapt up, nearly knocking the chair to the floor, and stormed out the double glass doors. Shaking my head, I walked out more calmly and before I reached my car, he was calling me. It was his turn to be triggered and he was just as rattled as I'd been in those early parking lot days.

"Oh my God!" he shouted, "If this is how I've been making you feel, I get it and I am so sorry. This sucks!" I took it all in and it was glorious. I told him as matter of fact, yes, that was exactly how I'd been feeling. Then he said that I got under his skin like no one else, and I knew exactly what he meant.

Just like the perfect storm, we were meant to be specifically this for each other at that time. The few years between leaving the job and meeting Rusty had been spent in personal growth work and I mistakenly believed the only purpose was to lose weight.

I had no idea exactly how far from my own truth I had been. This was bringing me to my knees and radiating out through my heart. And now it was his turn. Maybe it was an effort to feel powerful after being so down, or maybe he just mistook himself as more powerful than he was, but he made one fatal error by choosing to lie to my face. Instead of working out the back rent, he said he couldn't pay even the current rent. I gave him two weeks and he paid nothing.

I was indignant. I didn't understand how ungrateful and entitled it seemed he had become. That anger exploded into some very deep and dark stuff for me to work on with Sean about my dad, money, and fear. He had to go.

I was still angry, but Rusty wanted to meet for drinks. For a moment I stopped and thought about how peaceful it could be to be around each other again. It made me long for that peace with him, even for just a brief moment. But he'd gone too far. I was already well into planning his evection. I was resolute. He was stuck.

What followed were days of unrest. I wrestled with how far this had gone and how quickly. There was no time to care that my heart or soul would grieve deeply for this man. I could care less that we had a connection or what it was. I gave Dallas a call and listed the property for sale.

My most fabulous friend Kevin, who'd been monitoring my sanity all along, told me to come home to San Diego, which I did. While grateful for the warmth of his friendship and the stay in his beautiful home, even there I found no peace. I stayed ten days, but my mood only turned darker. The emotions were too big, too painful, and too overwhelming to even begin to process. When I returned, I got in the car and drove to Yellowstone. I had cousins living there who I had not met before, and they were gracious tour guides. But the energy of our fallout followed me all the way to the geysers. Nearly two years of my life had been spent around this man. He finally texted that he hated it when we didn't get along. Tears gushed over my cheeks as I replied the same.

Three weeks after the condo was in Escrow Rusty invited

me to breakfast. As I knew he would, Rusty popped out of his car with a grin on his face, just as he had when we'd met at the grocery store so long ago. My heart and soul craved the warmth of his hug. My logical brain had done its homework and knew better than to walk into his arms like nothing had happened.

The first half of breakfast was spent with his questions and attempts to turn it all around. The last half brought about the dull recognition of defeat. I had done some research and shared some things I'd realized about his personality, which were honestly quite shocking. There was nothing left to do but pick up the pieces of our individual lives.

In the end I walked away with a random six-minute recording of our conversation that my phone captured, all on its own, a last eerie and strange little memento.

In a fit of anger, or perhaps drunkenness that night I sent off a scathing email to him saying he would do nothing with his life but leave a wake of pain and heartbreak wherever he went. Strangely, that helped me process and release all of the anger, which left me again longing for that old peace between us. We exchanged a few half-hearted texts, but I'd finally managed to say enough to make even Rusty go quiet.

One morning as I listlessly returned home from a walk, I wandered through the lobby and peered into my small mailbox, and along came a curious piece of mail. It was addressed to Rusty at my address. Everything else dropped to the floor as I gripped this piece with both hands. Through the fog of confusion and exhaustion, it was too soon for me to be able to see this as a sign of things to come. Yet that's exactly what it was.

CHAPTER 33: LET'S ALL MOVE THEN

Disempowering the shadows of the heart.

Having picked up both my chin and the mail that had fallen to the floor I hopped into the elevator which lifted me up to my little abode. I shot him a text about the mail with no reply but a few weeks later it was a different mailbox that held news. An email arrived from Rusty announcing that he had gotten back together with his ex-girlfriend, and hoped I was doing well. All I could do was shake my head.

I spent a lot of time walking in the wooded trails around the area, letting songs drift lazily through my earbuds, which offered a sense of calm as the breeze rose off Puget Sound. I felt solo. And I was. The times I'd been able to spend with my son were less than a tenth of what I'd hoped and the few friends I'd made had their own busy lives, so the void left by Rusty was a large one. We had spent a lot of time together. I was surrounded by memories. It was worse than the breakup of an actual relationship because in so many strange and unbelievable ways it had seemed much closer. Which I guess had been the purpose all along.

The walls blocking my emotions had been demolished and my heart had come alive in ways I'd not expected possible, in a very different type of love, one that had awakened the awareness of my very soul. Everything on this journey I had unwillingly embarked upon, opened my eyes to how hidden my soul had been all along. Pieces of my life were unfolding now in ways I would have never understood before this.

I felt a void, but he wasn't gone. He'd constantly held a in place in my mind and my energy since that first glance when my words had escaped me. Recently my heart - right in the center - had begun to ache, deeply. It felt like the opposite of the overwhelming and loving sense of warmth I'd felt before. This was new, something I didn't understand and didn't much care for either.

Restlessness took me down to the waterfront where I found a mix of venues, a farmer's market, a brewery, retail shopping, restaurants, a gym along with a theater. For a moment I let myself wonder what it must be like to live in such a place that seemed to have it all. I'd been in my complex for over two years now and had really loved it.

Maybe it was the restlessness, but I couldn't get the idea of living there out of my head. The next day as I waited in line for a cup of coffee at a drive-thru Starbucks, I looked up the number for one of the buildings that had rental units at the waterfront and placed a call.

"Oh, that's so strange," said the man who answered as he explained just that morning he'd gotten a notice on a rare one bedroom. Would I like to see it? I smiled because I'd already planned to have coffee with Anshu at a café there the next morning.

We both loved it! The building had more outdoor space than ours. The interior walls were a lovely shade making it inviting and calm and everything looked shiny and new. It was more expensive, but it was quite an upgrade. Over coffee I shared with her the deep physical ache I'd been feeling in my heart. Anshu looked at me in a strange way and said she'd also felt something similar, like something was off.

We finished our coffees and headed home, and I was considering the move. As we pulled into the parking garage and were barely past the entry gate my foot slammed on the break. Oh my god! I turned to Anshu and pointed ahead where I saw Rusty's car parked in our garage. I pulled into a parking space but neither of us wanted to exit my vehicle.

Like two kids fearing a bully we called for Nana to come down to the garage for back up. Nana refused to believe it was his car. She inched closer and glanced in the window and there was a timesheet with his full name in plain view. Both the girls shrieked and headed for the elevator.

I understood because they knew about everything crazy that had already happened. I took the time and moved my car to another level in the garage. Anshu, not wanting to be alone, me not wanting to go home, and Nana in disbelief, all sat in Anshu's apartment next door to mine talking together just trying to make sense of it all.

When the eeriness stilled just a bit, I walked the few steps home where I found my Wi-Fi not working. Not one thing in my apartment would connect. I slumped onto the couch and followed every remedy to reset, restart and reboot but I was trapped in my little studio with no connection. Logically, I thought it must be a problem in the building, so I checked in with Nana, who was happily streaming Netflix.

Down to the second floor I went with my laptop and phone in tow, none of which worked at her place either. We both looked at each other and at the exact same moment both said he must be in the building.

Suddenly, I knew what was going on. He'd moved into our building. I knew why I'd gotten that piece of mail; it was like an advance warning. He'd put down my apartment number instead of his own. Suddenly, I knew why Anshu and I had felt that pain in our hearts.

The next morning, I felt like a stranger in my own building as I snuck down to the office. The lovely woman I'd come to know and really liked registered the panic on my face as I explained my situation. Without violating anyone's privacy, she confirmed our fears, Rusty, his girlfriend, and their daughter were our new neighbors.

By the grace of God, I had already been provided a way out. I didn't want to run away like a coward, but I couldn't shake the eeriness I felt. I was ready to sign the lease in the new building. As I got to my car I noticed the driver's side valve stem cover had been removed along with the center rim cover. Since Rusty had been the one to replace all four of them for me, this had his name all over it. Like a message, even if you try to hide-I still found you. I shook my head and silently thanked God for the ability to move.

I can't explain this type of energy, but it did seem like it made sparks fly it was so intense. With the paperwork done I still had to wait a few weeks to move, which was unnerving. I didn't understand. I felt like I was being stalked but knew that wasn't the case.

Amazingly, just as the new place had come at the exact right time, so did the next solution, almost as if to say not to lose faith. Remy, who had just booked a trip to Bali called to ask if I wanted to join her for part of it! The timing was perfect, and I couldn't wait.

As if my soul had called out for what it needed next,

I couldn't have made a better choice myself that the beautifully healing shelter of Bail. Just getting away from that building, heading to SeaTac, and boarding that outbound plane brought renewed peace.

Looking for an Airbnb in Bali is like shopping for paradise. Our first was lush and tropical, with a gorgeous pool, outdoor showers, and exquisite beauty. More so than Belize, everything was geared towards bringing nature inside. This land and the people of Ubud, the town where we stayed, held such reverence for both humanity and the planet.

As Remy and I visited the landscapes filled with lavish rice patties, gardens, and temples, we learned that the peaceful energy of the people centered around family and faith. Each day they awoke and went to temple, located right in their home. The family unit was fully intact, living in compound-style accommodations, three generations at a time, together. No need for child or elder care, and decisions were made on behalf of everyone, not just one person. The beauty was in the embrace of their natural acceptance of each other. We saw only one beauty salon, probably meant for us tourists. At times we saw women carrying beautiful baskets stacked several high on top of their heads, who smiled as we drove alongside them. These were people who could fit more on a scooter than I could in my car.

We spent our days visiting several local healers, water temples, the Elephant and Monkey sanctuaries and filling our bellies with simple, healthy fresh meals. The only thing that pulled me back into my life before Bali was the day Remy asked me, "Dude, what's up with you and electronics?" and I knew she was right.

I'd been unable to use an ATM, turn on a stereo, start a movie or do a simple transfer of photos no matter what method I tried. She had no problem with any of it. So, as we sat over dinner that evening, I filled her in on the latest part of that journey. Whatever electrified energy was created in the connection I had with Rusty, it seemed to go berserk with all the recent changes between us. Remy, who had just finished a cocktail that filled a pineapple shook her head and ordered a second.

In honor of her upcoming birthday, Remy and I changed Airbnb's and the new one was right in the middle of a jungle, a structure made of all natural woods and stones. Koi fish swam around our feet as we followed the steppingstones to enter the courtyard. This property could have slept a dozen of our friends had we brought them along. I had a house with three bedrooms as Remy took the lower level flat next to the pool. What a great place that would have been for a pandemic! And both of those homes were less expensive than our daily rent at home.

Bali opened my eyes to the balance and inner peace found when families operate in unconditional love, acceptance and kindness. Rusty had opened my eyes to so many things but the latest were a strong sense of boundaries. He's shown me clear indicators of the unacceptability of things I'd once considered normal. I went home unafraid of all the change.

I got back in time for my son's 40th tiki themed birthday party and moved into the new building a few days later. Once again my electronics went haywire.

CHAPTER 34:
BLESSINGS ARE
ALL AROUND

Healing is just a thought away.

Leaving Rusty behind was not leaving Rusty. His energy remained with me, as did the feelings left behind for me to work through. I questioned all that had happened and relentlessly sought out the hidden pain that cried out for healing. The signs, coincidences, and reminders moved into the new place with me. Whether I was signing up at the gym or looking for an editor I was finding people who had experienced similar soul connections.

At a bar in the new building a young man turned in my direction and started up a conversation with me. He turned out to also be an electrician, who at one time, had been Rusty's coach. He was very freaked out and paranoid that I knew him. Whatever Rusty's deal was, I was clearly not the only one impacted by him in some very strange ways.

I continued working on my childhood trauma with Sean and at the end of one meeting I saw these giant crystals. I had no idea why or what they meant but when my friend Alexis wanted to go to a crystal shop a few days later, I was not surprised.

As we browsed around the owner of the shop offered to show us the upper level and there we found, guess what… a room totally filled with crystals. As we passed the room I placed my hand on the center of my chest and gasped because a steady pressure was building there. She asked if we wanted to take a peek in at the crystals but by now I was having a very difficult time breathing. I asked her if anyone had died in that room. This was too similar to not ask. She quickly denied it but when the pressure in my chest increased she finally shared the fact that her son had died, but again, reassured it hadn't happened there. I asked how he had died and sure enough he'd been crushed to death. His chest had collapsed in the exact spot I was feeling the pain.

And then my jaw began to ache. Out of the blue I asked if she had anything to say to her son. Alexis looked like a deer in headlights. The woman refused, saying she'd made peace with him, but from what I was feeling I doubted that her son was resting peacefully. Heading to the car I grabbed my phone and searched for a spiritual reason for my jaw to tighten up like this and read that this happens when a voice has been stifled. It stayed like that for four hours.

The blessing was I was no longer terrified. It seems as there must be more than we think to life, and I just happened to be able to tune in at times. The beauty of it was I understood enough to not panic.

Sometimes putting our desires out there in the energy bring them about. When I'd wanted a new friend to walk with I meant Jolyne less than a minute later. When I wanted to take a boat ride for my birthday and couldn't find anyone to join me I met Sue and Jerry who were celebrating their anniversary the same day. Wishing I knew more people in the area I met Kim and Paul as they were leaving a pub I frequented.

And the signs that point to a deeper meaning in meeting Rusty don't end either. For a while I kept seeing things that somehow reminded me of my childhood phone number only to look at the full number and realize it was his birthdate. There are dozens of parallels in birthdates of family members as well as places we've both randomly visited that cannot be explained.

Through it all, I did my best to adapt. I was enjoying my new apartment except for one thing; the vending machines in the lobby became a beacon of dysfunction. Gradually, hypnotherapy helped. I was eating better and had far fewer moments that went out of control. The more I processed and released the more it lessened my anxiety and the need for outside distraction to feel safe and calm.

It was in this home in that new building that I learned to master the art of tracking back triggers. So many times, I'd pass by those vending machines and not think twice about them. But there they sat, with their massive steel and glass, mini versions of a seven eleven, waiting for a moment of uncertainty. One particular night after a lovely evening out with Alexis and her husband, I couldn't walk past those machines. The next day I called my coach pal Tom to discuss, and he asked what had been different about that night than any other.

This is the thing about triggers; they snake their way in and go unnoticed left lurking in the darkness, playing with you as long as they possibly can. They take you out of consciousness and drag you into limbo between conscious and subconscious thoughts. A limbo created by one moment that you must be able to find in order to find your way out. Tom's question was the one thing I needed to get me thinking again in a conscious state and I remembered exactly what the trigger had been. As we were leaving I told my friends to call me once in a while because it seemed I was the one to reach out most often.

Uncovering that moment led to the emotion that the one simple comment had evoked, which was an old feeling of being unwanted. I already knew where the root of that was. Sometimes the core root of a false belief can have many memories attached to it but often clearing a major one can break it's hold and remove its ability to trigger. Like this next one.

The reflection of the blazing sun bounced off the side mirror, landing directly in the eyes of the little girl, blinking harshly. Trying to dislodge the spots that had formed to block her vision she looked eagerly towards her mother who sat in the driver's seat of the vehicle. With excited energy the girl hopped from the car, walking towards the hospital entrance, excited to see the family friend they'd come here to visit. Her mom, strangely quiet, lead the child down the sterile hallways and into an open door. The girl, expecting to see a friend, instead found herself in an office. She was asked to take a seat. Her mother sat in the chair next to her.

A sturdy woman sat behind an equally sturdy desk, looking official and making the little girl tense. Her body upright, her lips began to quiver as she tuned into the conversation which was about her. Many of the words made no sense, but she knew she'd not heard the friends name once.

Something was wrong. No one seemed happy to be here, which made her confused. With that the child was handed off to a woman wearing all white. As she looked back, her mother kept getting smaller and smaller and her waves finally stopped altogether. The little girl was taken to a large room, asked to put on a strange costume and told to climb into a large bed-like object. The woman in white pulled up a hidden side of the bed so a railing snapped into place making a terrifying noise as it did. And then she was left alone with no way to reach the tissue or means to quell her sobbing.

The adult in me could still hear Sean's voice. Instinctively I knew I was safe, and, in that safety, the quiet fear gave way to guttural moaning, unleashing a flood of tears I feared may drown me.

What happened next, what I remember happening next was glancing up to find my parents, both standing at the foot of the hospital bed where I'd been imprisoned.

I saw myself there, in the tiny child's body, startled by the sudden bellowing, the fear being released in angry shrieks. The woman in white was begging her parents to intervein; the same parents who'd been content in deferring all responsibility to the hospital (and were perhaps hopeful it may have been relinquished for good).

From my groggy state of hypnosis, my one and possibly only time of childhood empowerment came to light as I shared with Sean the story of the Tressy doll. The nurse, clearly distressed, fearing the stiches from my tonsillectomy would become as unraveled as I had, strongly suggested the use of bribery.

Somehow my brain had put together the fact that my parents were not trustworthy and for a moment I had the power of leverage. For the adults to get what they wanted, I had to be given that doll. Now, not later, because like the swim lessons, I knew the doll would not appear. My dad grudgingly left the hospital and returned with the toy. And that was the one and only time I remember actually choosing something for myself that hadn't been handed down from my cousins. There had been another doll in my past, the last of her kind because I'd gotten in so much trouble for cutting the hair off her head. Redemption was mine that day, a second grader who was smart enough now to ask for a doll who's hair could grow back!

Every trapped emotion wants it day in the sunshine.

Photo: Doll with a haircut

CHAPTER 35: ALL THINGS AS THEY ARE MEANT TO BE

What you want matters, even if you don't learn that until later in life.

Life was going to keep me moving.

When I'd first come to town William was on his own, but his girlfriend had moved to town and in with him, which meant even less free time for me and a new dynamic. Let's just say I had enough free time that I visited San Diego often enough that I was the first person my friend Greg thought of when he needed a house sitter. He and his wife were about to take to the road in an RV. Since they would be gone about three months, Greg's wife, Mar Sue, suggested that I find a traveling nurse to sublet my place to save on expenses, which worked out just fine.

About a week in, bright and early one morning I got a call from Greg. Groggily looking at the phone, it suddenly occurred to me that I may be homeless if they were coming back. That summer ended up having a lot of surprises in store for me which included not one but two other people in the house than expected, two different issues with automobiles and some serious surprise construction.

But I learned a lot about myself and how to accommodate the unexpected. I learned that having the ability to make informed decisions for myself is paramount in my life. But most importantly I learned that I had a long way to go. I had come there thinking I was a rock-solid human but the thing about personal growth work is it is never-ending. We can continually learn more about ourselves which can lead to us be better people.

I took a drive to my favorite little beach town within the city and sat out on the jetty. I called Anshu as the ocean roared in the background and told her how much I loved it there. I said I could see myself being happy in a small apartment right there by the ocean. After my experience renting out that condo, I was far less interested in owning a home again. Maybe that opened a door in the universe for a move back to San Diego because shortly after some friends started talking with me about a possible job. Here I was, after two years of busting down doors to find employment, with a potential job offer, several years later. You just never know.

I was on the verge of turning the big 6-OH and for the first time I really wanted to celebrate me! Because it fell on a busy holiday weekend, Tiffany smartly insisted we book a place months in advance. I had picked this cute little hippy beach town for the celebration long before Greg's house-sitting gig came up.

Brad and Tiff had rented a beach cottage for my birthday. I am beyond grateful for the incredibly generous and wonderful people in my life. Honestly, I'm not sure I deserve many of the people I've had in my life because I've been an asshole to more than just my son. Maybe there are some people who can see deep down when you are a product of pain rather than just a horrible person, or maybe all horrible people are products of pain. As they say, hurt people hurt people.

I wished I could have been where I was at sixty when I'd turned forty-nine because my friends, and even my boss, threw quite an extravaganza that year for me. I'm talking about a boat rental on the bay for about forty people, fully catered and I arrived by limo.

My emotions were so shut down back then, I didn't know how to appreciate it nearly as much as I should have. My heart was too heavily protected at that time.

And truthfully I paid a heavy price. It was my friend Emma who'd planned that party and eventually she completely turned her back on me, at a time when I had no way of understanding why. Which is why digging so deeply into our pasts seems to be so crucial to our own happiness. Until we free ourselves of pain we can easily create it. I drastically lacked filters and had no fear of conflict; couple that with a lack of empathy and I was certain to piss some people off. Emotional awareness truly is the path to mindfulness. I haven't stopped missing Emma and her mom and probably never will. But, the truth is, emotionally shut down people may not form true friendships. I think there had to be a disconnect for a friendship to have been so easily disposable.

Turning sixty looked so different from where I was for my 49th birthday. I seriously thought about what I wanted, which was something I was still getting used to. I made a list of things we could do and shot it out to people without pressure or expectations. Those four days were as low-key and incredible as they come. We started out on Friday night with a group of us going on a harbor cruise, which could not have been better. The next day we invited everyone for a beach day followed by a bonfire. On Sunday we gathered for lunch and ended at the Comedy Store. And as a birthday dinner we walked down to the local Pizza Port for a meal followed by a decadent chocolate cake. Every moment in between was packed with fun, laughter, and adventure, but most importantly, I was in the most amazing company ever.

As Brad and I were out walking to get a coffee one

morning I shared with him what I had been saying to Anshu, about how I thought I could live there. It's an eclectic hippy scene which speaks to my very soul. He was the last to leave that weekend and dropping him off at the airport nearly broke me. My heart had opened so much.

In my mind I knew that everyone who contributed to my 49th cared for me. But on my 60th I felt the love deep in my heart and soul. What a blessing to have many of the same people at both. I had to be grateful for all of the recent experiences that had blown my heart wide open because I am certain without them I would have not experienced the depth of love I felt then and have felt every day since.

My friends Andrew and Mary joined us Pizza Port and officially asked me to come work for them! It would make flying home bittersweet. While we hadn't shaken hands and we were all expecting I'd take the job, I just wanted to talk with William first. There had been too many times his life had gotten caught up in his families and I was doing all I could to not mess up any further.

William and I had gone on a few short road trips, taken in some movies and enjoyed some nice meals out. And it was certainly wonderful to celebrate the holidays together. I'd broken down in regret and tearful apologies countless times. I had given everything I could think of to make amends. But there were no magical words to make

William trust me enough to bring me close again.

I understand what it feels like when you can't give your parents that privilege. It was why I didn't invite my mom to my last wedding. I wanted the day without fear of what she might say to upset me. I didn't even bother take her health seriously enough as her days came to an end. Maybe that last summer before William's senior year had broken something in him when it came to me. Maybe my own actions had taught him to think of me the same way as I had thought of his grandmother. Certainly, the fact that my mom had left her own son behind had influenced my choices.

So, what I had hoped would happen, what I wanted most seemed impossible. I wanted the bond I hadn't had with my own parents. I didn't expect it. But I wanted to have a close relationship with my son where we could talk openly and honestly about most things.

The bullshit I had endured during my own childhood that left me so walled up and emotionally unavailable had created too deep of a rift and the truth was he may never find a way to trust me again emotionally.

I don't know how to get a family on the same page once this type of damage has been done. I was in my fifties before I could even clue in, so I doubt I would have been open to anything either of my parents might have had to say. At least not before I found my way back to an empathic place in my own heart.

So, I committed to the move back to San Diego. I was again in the business of selling everything I owned. What I had put out into the cosmos about living by the beach with Brad and Anshu manifested into a furnished rental right across the street from the sand in my favorite little hippy town.

My heart broke leaving William.

I finally felt the love and honesty in what my mom had written to me in her books. I knew what she meant because I knew that William would probably not truly know the depth of my love for him. A mother's love for her children is like no other. But let me take that back. The truth is a mother who's heart is open has love for her children like no other. Everything I'd felt during that time with Rusty now paled in comparison in what I felt for my only child. But I had needed the unearthing all this had brought so the frail and tattered remnants of my heart could finally break free from the bonds of all the bullshit baggage I'd carried around, to be open again.

If only our innocence as children could be protected for as long as it needs to be. If we could live in the safety of the warm unconditional embraces of our caregivers, being guided gently, loved, and supported fully, I believe we would have the foundation we need to thrive and succeed as adults. If we had that safe, accepting, non-judgmental place where we are free to become who we truly want to be, where our mistakes do not turn into character assassinations but are instead teaching moments, we can find balance in life. To get that, parents have to find a way to fiercely seek out true emotional self-awareness.

But for me, for William, and for pretty much everyone else, it's a lot more like running a track meet without training or proper shoes and still being expected to win. Childhoods filled with confusion, conditioning, and pain that breeds fear don't make for a smooth landing into adulthood. We carry unknown anxiety we can't access and lack the tools to process or understand our own emotions because no one who came before us understood theirs either. Which, I guess is why we remain like ships passing in the night, rather than family.

CHAPTER 36: THE SEA, THE SUN, THE SAND, AND THE RELEASE

The most important relationship is the one you have with yourself.

While the trip up the coast had taken weeks, the one down took only two days and the odometer in my car read 222,222 on arrival! On day three I reported to my new place of employment. My friends were happy to have me around, kind, generous and a big part of more of my healing. Because of them, I focused more on where I wanted to live rather than the cost which was why I had found a place across the street from the ocean.

The first thirty years I'd lived in San Diego had been nowhere close to the water. It's weird how living even fifteen minutes away tends to put the ocean in the back of your mind, or at least it had for me. I had been conditioned to believe that money was more important than I was as a kid and that what I wanted didn't matter. It was no wonder my decisions were made without a thought to whether I'd be happy or not. It was no wonder I couldn't enjoy those fabulous experiences or appreciate my 49th birthday, because I had felt for so long that I didn't matter.

And you know that's the really shitty thing about situations like this. There was not one day when I felt like I had an issue with self-worth because I felt very worthy. I felt like I had value...right up until I lost the job that had falsely served as security. In other words, I only felt like I mattered when it seemed like what I was doing mattered. Which, by the way, makes it really hard to know if you have any issues to work on at all.

What began as being physically near death was the death of all that bullshit. I was finally beginning to trust myself and know that my own emotional self-awareness was well on its way and that I had all that I needed to keep myself safe.

But even with the move the lessons and the growth were still coming from my soul's connection to Rusty. Right on schedule all my electronics at the beach acted up for a month as well as wreaking havoc at the new office. And almost as if to say, you are not there yet bitch, the most blatant reminder happened on the freeway.

Usually, I can make my way through any kind of traffic, but one day, I remember saying to myself, man I just can't get away from this. When this stuff happens, there is usually a reason and sure enough a few minutes later a truck cut across a lane, got right in front of me and slowed down. Frustrated I slowed as well, and that's when I saw it. The license plates on that truck were Rusty's birthday in the exact order of month, day, and year. Was there no escape? A few weeks later when a credit card replacement arrived, there it was again the numbers appeared in the same exact order all over again.

Those experiences had shown me a complete and total vulnerability which I'd not experienced before. For the first time I let someone see me fully without fear of judgement or rejection. I believe when we meet a soul connection of this magnitude, we each appear to the other as needed for maximum personal growth and the connection remains in order for that to continue. This, I believe, is unconditional love in its original form.

With the move and new job, I had landed in a safe place, one of love and acceptance. Even so, after just a few short months my friends and I all agreed this job wasn't for me at this time. Like many of the experiences in my life this too seemed to have a purpose geared towards a change of direction.

Returning to the industry I'd left behind wasn't what I

was here for. I still had more of my own work to do, and I was now in a place where my focus could be totally on me. I continued with Sean, using the numbers on the scale and my ability to control my food as our guidelines. And like those last months in the house, I knew what I was doing wasn't sustainable.

Living right on the water in a furnished place was the vacation my soul needed. Brad said I had called it to myself. Being so close to the ocean is a constant source of amazement for which I am eternally grateful. So often I think had I lived here during my first San Diego life I may not have wanted to leave and take the journey I have. But now I wonder if it's taken this long for another reason. Like the rest of the incredible things I've experienced, would this too have been lost on me back then?

As a year approached I began looking around for another less expensive option and what an amazing blessing it has been to have moved before the pandemic and housing shortages. My buddy Koungie who had helped me unpack my car when I came back now offered to help me move along with Remy and even stayed long enough to help put together some furniture. True friends are the best and I'm so grateful for all of mine. My new place is a short walk to the beach just two blocks away. It was here I'd face down the stuff I needed to do alone. I was no longer in temporary housing, and I had to face what that meant.

A few months after the move I went back up north for a visit. It was close enough to the holidays I thought we could have an early Thanksgiving celebration which ended in disaster. While out shopping with William's girlfriend our discussion became heated. Heated enough that she chose to throw me out of their house. As I left to get a hotel room I went over the conversation with her and the one I had with my son afterwards in my mind and between the two I felt very confused. My son seemed happy I'd agreed to leave and while we met for lunch again before I left there was no resolve, which happens when emotional walls get in the way. They had both told me I should keep things "surface" (a place I was long past) so all I could do was enact a few boundaries, accept the situation for what it was and set it aside. So, I worked on the things I could.

The connection I'd felt with Rusty was still all around me, signs were everywhere, and each brought up a memory or a feeling, so this is what I dug into. At this point, I was tuning into how **I felt about things rather than how things made me feel** and I wanted at least one of the situations from the Pacific Northwest to have some resolve.

I know it sounds absolutely insane if you've not had something like this in your life, but this is what I was working with. From my research for many it's a connection that must end as a romance but for me there was a draw that had meaning that I wanted to get to the bottom of. Even if what we had was an eternal connection, we were living separate lives and while I was fine with that mentally, maybe some part of me hadn't made peace with that just yet.

As I thought about what nagged at me the most it was a weird combination of loss and hope. Because that experience had opened up my heart so deeply and felt like nothing I'd felt before I had kept a small piece of hope that I'd see him again. So, I turned back to myself and asked what exactly was it that was missing that I couldn't give to myself. Sure, putting love out in the world is good but what about putting some right back into your own heart? If I was still dysfunctional with how I ate I was not demonstrating self-love.

It was that sliver of hope blocking my way. I realized what I needed to do was face the brutal truth, it was likely I would not see Rusty again in this life. Since I knew I'd visit my son in the area, I must have been holding hope that I'd see him again. Hope still had me clinging to one more big, huge grin directed right at me, and my soul ached for one more gigantic hug. I didn't want to be with him, but I really didn't want to be without him and that was the issue.

Hope had been keeping me stuck. Identifying that was the very first step. You need to be certain of what you specifically have to face. And then you must process the pain, look into why it's so painful, what meaning it holds because as long as you cling to its meaning you will stay stuck in that space. It had been something I felt I needed, to be able to keep the connection alive in person, because I didn't trust that the depth of the soul connection would be enough.

It was just like that fucking stuffed avocado! I was deeply afraid I would disappear again without being able to reach him. This work was deeper than the emotional cleansing from childhood, this was a soul cleansing. So, just as I had done when I learned to be alone, I sat by myself and grieved my loss. I took all of those ideas that others were projected about being together and drilled down on what I really wanted instead. I let my soul wail out loud in angst. I didn't need hypnosis to reach the pain, it came right on out and flowed like a river of tears.

I cried until I knew I was going to be just fine if we didn't cross paths again. Just as I'd learned in the past life regression with Sean. And now I could trust myself enough now to know this was true. The pieces we unravel fall in the order they need to for us to finally understand. And then I sat in prayer. I asked God to receive Rusty back into his arms and protect him. I released him back to the beautiful energy of all that surrounds us all in peace and loving kindness.

That's what made me realize the love I was feeling was more about myself than anyone else. Whatever the reason we connect so deeply with another at times does seem to have a mission and for me the mission was giving myself back to me. When it first began everything seemed so tied to him, but with this release I understood how it all pointed right back to me, which was where the journey had been meant to take me anyway. The mission was to remove each piece of pain and fear so I would stop self-sabotaging and be kind to myself and others. The mission was to live with compassion and empathy. I'd found the truth for myself.

And then, I got a phone call from Rusty one night. It had been three years since I'd seen him and I was happy to hear he was doing so well, he'd cleared up his credit, gotten a promotion at his work and bought himself a house and was still in a relationship. But he also said he'd called because he wanted to see me. I told him I'd moved, and he wanted to know when I would be back...after a half hour we said our goodbyes. And the next day I was angry.

There was no reason for me to be angry at Rusty, he was just being the person I'd known him to be all along. So I processed our call and let that shit go in gratitude that I'd done the work to be fine letting him go. But the anger continued and took me to a deeper place. The timing was spot on for the next piece of cleansing. Anger, full-fledged anger had surfaced a few times around him, but I'd later realize that it hadn't come up much in my work with Sean.

For some reason, that call prompted me to sit down and write a letter to my parents for the first time ever. The letter read like an outline of my life. It was absolutely shocking to see the list of things I disliked about my childhood had become my life's direction. ALL OF IT. Which makes it even more shocking that most of us don't give childhood any thought at all. I studied that list at length. I shouted, I huffed, I threw stuff, and I broke down and sobbed because it was so clear where everything that had blocked me, held me up, left me feeling less than, unwanted, in the way and made me a horrible parent had all begun in that home. Every piece of pain, fear, confusion, every false belief had come from there.

It let me off the hook for all the stuff that had not been my fault in the first place. I had been so busy carrying around all the shame and guilt from those years while there was no time, training, or tools to take on the real responsibility for myself. All the anxiety I'd carried forward throughout my lifetime, all the responsibility I'd taken for my unpreparedness and social ineptness fell away in a flood of tears the poured out for hours.

We want to believe that we naturally have self-awareness and self-love but just like empathy they are not innate.

They all get shoved into the background as we climb into the little pod we ride thru life in. You cannot possibly fully love who you are when you carry around a bunch of bullshit beliefs about what, how and who you are that were projected upon you without your consent. At best you can do what I did and pretend to like who you are by just not caring what people think.

Again, I went back to work with Sean. Our job together was to finish unpacking the emotional baggage in my subconscious so I could free space to be conscious and mindful and then move into spiritual growth from there. I suspiciously wondered if all the crazy weird stuff had been a test to see if I'd jump ahead of what I was ready for. Sometimes spiritual beliefs have a way of keeping you stuck in your own ego and thinking you know more than you do, I did not want to go there if I could avoid it.

CHAPTER 37: NO HEART BREAKS LOUDER THAN A MOM'S

Neither parents or children ever fully know the extent of their effects on each other.

In the middle of the pandemic, after months of sheltering safely, I found myself boarding a plane. All the fear I'd had about this virus fell away when I'd gotten a call from my son the night before. He told me I was gonna want to come up for a visit. Every ounce of my body froze in fear and panic. For twenty-five years I had dreaded the thought of getting a call about his health, but this was one that had not crossed my mind.

I wanted to be a rock for my boy but when I heard William's next words I crumbled. Any strength and calm I'd hoped to exhibit drained along with the color in my face as my child told me he was in the hospital preparing to possibly lose his foot. I asked as many questions as I could as a horrifying shriek welled up inside. Tears now falling like rain onto my lap. I clung to even the tiniest shred of hope listening to him speak. My mind sprang into action seeking ways he could best advocate for himself, wanting desperately for my only child's body to remain whole. I assured him I'd get on the first possible flight. He said he was tired, so we said our good-byes.

A howling shriek came out of my body as I balled up on the floor and cried uncontrollably. Never, in my life, had pain or grief cut into my soul in this way.

After years of being barricaded behind walls of denial, empathy seemed to be ganging up to pounce on me now. Just the very thought of your own child having to go through this is unkindly surreal. I couldn't imagine how he must be feeling.

My parental instinct was no longer missing in action. I wanted it to be me instead. I prayed the prayers of the desperate begging that whatever it was be given to me. I would do anything. I'd trade myself fully if God would just protect William.

I spent the next hours rushing around organizing myself for travel and extended time away. The flight I'd booked left at 6:00 am but sleep was impossible. I'd been on the phone with friends who did all they could to be supportive. There was nothing left to do but pace and wait until I could call an Uber for a ride to the airport. A few hours later at the check-in counter I looked at my boarding pass and noticed the date. It was Rusty's birthday. WTF.

Nothing felt more significant than this. My heart was now shredded in grief and my mind raced in doubt of what was to come. Fortunately, there had been enough of a lull in the pandemic that the hospital allowed visitors, unfortunately it was only one person per day, so I had to coordinate with William's girlfriend Mandy to take turns… and I had not spoken to her in close to a year.

When I phoned my walking buddy Jolyne to let her know I'd be in town she told me to stay with her, which was an amazing blessing. She, along with a lot of her family, have been wonderful friends since the day we met. I know she really wanted to help me and was worried about keeping me busy to keep my mind off things, while I was just worried about falling apart. I was a terrible guest, all I could do, for weeks on end, was curl up in bed and process the pain and fear one step at a time. While trying to avoid Covid.

After dozens of desperate texts, Mandy finally realized just how little I knew and called to update me. She told me that William had not been waiting to possibly have foot surgery, as he'd said. He'd actually already had three surgeries. The day I arrived they had amputated mid-thigh above the knee of his right leg. This was by far the most shocked and stunned I'd been in my life.

After that last visit, when I'd been asked to leave their home, I had backed away. I was an unwanted part of the family, something I was all too familiar with from my past. Even though I had learned that he had type 2 diabetes, I stayed out of things and stopped asking questions.

All I can comfortably share is how this experience affected me. I had to process how I felt about what this meant for my son and his future. I had to process how I felt about the exclusion I was experiencing. And I had to try and remain positive for seven weeks as I visited. I wanted to spend every possible second that was offered to me with my boy.

Acceptance, while generally a very beautiful thing, can be a really hard pill to swallow at times. I offered help which was consistently refused. I was quietly being left out in the cold. I now had to find acceptance in the knowledge that doing the work to become a better person didn't mean I'd be treated any differently than I was when I was acting like a dick.

A fully open heart is tough to maintain. We still have to protect ourselves with boundaries in order to survive when things overwhelm. And even though I'd shed more tears in a few short years than I had in the past six decades, I was grateful to not be emotionally shut down, even then.

It seemed maybe I was destined to be stuck between two generations who just didn't want to talk about their feelings. I think our subconscious works against us in so many ways and this is one. As it hides us away from repressed pain it hides us from ourselves and others.

Maybe our family has been burdened with resentment. My parents, or at least my dad resented that I'd even been born. And the way he treated me because of it had caused me to dislike neediness in others. Being needy in the home I grew up in was useless, it was a reason to be shamed. Needing something put you in the way which was a bad place to be. The message I got was that needing anything from my parents made me a bad person. Which turned me into an overly responsible person.

The false belief that neediness was bad and the lack of empathy that my own emotional shutdown caused made it impossible for me to accept my son's needs as a child. What an incredibly horrible realization to come to. I had gotten no time at all to unravel any of that before becoming his mother.

My son wanted, needed, and deserved what every child does, unconditional love and acceptance along with a safe and secure place to learn and grow. But in my cluelessness I turned around and shamed my own son for wanting what no one had given me because I had been shamed for wanting those things too.

If I could change just one thing in this world it would be the criteria for becoming a parent. I'd magically create an internal gauge so everyone could sense the level of emotional self-awareness needed before being entrusted with the precious innocent little lives of children. I think that could change the entire world. Because the cycles we are all repeating with this type of generational trauma, lack of individual emotional awareness and training to manage our feelings is wreaking havoc on us all. It blocks us from the truth. It blocks us from love.

Love is such a pure thing, so simple, it's just love. When we see the innocence of a baby or a puppy it's hard for most of us not to smile with joy and love in that moment. Maybe because they are so much closer to our creator, or a place where we know we are all connected, but a feeling of love is hard to miss at those times.

I believe we crave a return to that innocence, that purity, that love. True love is not something filled with desire or need. Love doesn't have expectations. True, pure, innocent love doesn't say you must be this way or that and it doesn't say you must be with me. Love, when unconditional, is just love. Without restraint. Love is at the core of each of us.

This is how I must love my son now, totally without

expectation. This is how I wish I'd been allowed to love him from his very first breath.

The true beauty of a soul connection like a twin soul is not in desperation or a longing desire for a worldly connection, but in acknowledging the depth of your soul how unnecessary that truly is. And had it not been for that experience I doubt I would have found this understanding for myself about my son.

CHAPTER 38: BRACE YOURSELF

Fear is not the enemy, avoiding it is.

As I neared the end and as time came closer to releasing this book…I panicked. Rereading it a final time I questioned everything. Was I sharing way too much. Was I sharing too much weird crap. Was I protecting everyone in how I said things. Would what I had written even matter to just one person.

For about ten days I was anxious and couldn't pinpoint exactly why. I went back to the methods I've been using to trace anxiety and made a list of everything that could be bothering me. I did the work around those things…still anxious. So, I turned back to journaling.

The magic of putting pen to paper (or fingers to keyboard!) is a load-lightener like no other really. There is something about taking some of the things that rattle around in your head and releasing them to the written word that is both a release and a relief. On paper you can scream without fear of being heard, you can shout, and no one will know or think twice about it. You can tell the page your truest, deepest trials and tragedies and it will subtlety guide your tear-filled eyes to the nearest tissue box. Here we can tell off our best friend, confess love unrequited, ask for help, let our parents or partners know when we have felt entirely let down and even offer our sincere gratitude for things long past to those who only live in our hearts. And somehow, magically almost, we make space to see things differently than before we sat down to write. We can sort more aptly what may still need to be said and even gain confidence and agency to share what still lingers. And it's between just us, you know. The journal you trust keeps your secrets and allows you to feel what you need and eventually say what's most important.

In 2015 I opened a word document and started writing. That doc has taken me through almost all of this journey and been one of the most important assets I've had to identify and process all that's happened. But nothing came out this time. It wasn't until I was standing in the shower the next morning that I got it. The clarity I needed washed over me like the cleansing spray of water rinsing away the panic. This had nothing to do with pain or hurt leftover from the past and nothing that was happening in my life has been the source. This anxiety was because of something that was new to me, new because of the changes I'd made.

Most of my life had been lived in something like a fortified little pod I'd created for myself, posing as the person I'd been molded into, and part of that mold was an I don't give a shit attitude. When my parents body shamed me at such a young age the message I'd received had been that no one was to be trusted, which translated into it wasn't safe to care what anyone thought about me.

Now, I was facing a new kind of vulnerability. I hadn't recognized my problem because it was a new one. All of those questions about the book had been the source of this new anxiety and I hadn't given them the light of day. Probably because they just seemed like such normal questions. But what I forgot was I had taken myself out of the pod and become vulnerable in ways I'd not been for most of my life.

I am dyslexic. I have been raised by wolves. All my life people have thought I should know more than I had been taught. I deeply lacked awareness. At times I had been a shit parent, partner, and friend. There were a lot of really weird, crazy, and strange things that I encountered. To share my story, I had to lay not only my soul bare but my heart open. I have to hope that we can communicate beyond belief systems and talk about truths that can help all of us.

As I toweled off and dug a little deeper it wasn't

necessarily the fear of judgement from releasing what I'd written that had been the problem. The anxiety was from fearing that fear. I hadn't stopped to look at any concern I may have about what people may say. I thought if I did I may just stop writing altogether. I'd shoved that fear under the rug in fear it would take me down. I was letting all of that get out in front of me.

As I've traveled this path it seems all roads have led to the one central theme of peace. Even the places of discomfort which bring the greatest growth, those have either pointed to lessons or pointed out that it was time to move on. We have to be comfortable enough with ourselves to get out of our comfort zone when needed. The anxiety I felt for those ten days was because I let go of the main theme, I'd let go of the knowledge that I was safe in the moment.

Fearing the fear of what might happen put me at odds with what I was doing. And that could have changed my entire direction or inhibited how I was doing things. Anxiety takes us off course and becomes a detour away from peace. All I had done was fallen right back into the same old trap of **wasting time seeking future security which left me feeling unsafe in the moment.**

And that's the rabbit hole of life in some societies. A gigantic loop spent seeking more while pretending to be something we are not because the truth of who we

really are buried so deeply under pain and insecurity. If we dare to look deep isn't the root of jealousy and conflict found in insecurity? When we react instead of responding calmly doesn't it have roots in pain or fear?

I had learned that all we need to turn this all around is a better emotional understanding of ourselves. Knowing how to manage our own emotions also leads to a higher capacity of acceptance and compassion for ourselves and others. But when we keep seeking fulfilment outside of ourselves we keep ourselves in a constant state of need. We don't carry our own power; we give it away to all the places/people/things we seek. We remain unbalanced.

I gave twenty-seven years to a job and a group of people who barely said goodbye as they shoved me out the door. I watched my parents be so fearful of running out of money I made making it the most important thing in my life. It made me believe that professional responsibility was more important that having personal responsibility to myself and my own child.

The inner peace so many have sought, and even sustainable happiness both have some pre-requisites. Putting a sign on your wall with a positive message doesn't make you more sustainably positive. Meditating in the morning doesn't do anything for you in the moments you become embroiled in conflict during the day. Just as eating a full meal at the dinner table doesn't mean you won't amble into the kitchen for a bowl of ice cream to go with your favorite late-night show.

The pre-requisite is the emotional self-awareness that leads to a conscious and balanced life. Life is meant to flow through us, this is where peace is found, in the flow of life. When life flows around us we stand in our own way blocking our peace. The roadblocks are rooted in the past. Past hidden pain and fear creating insecurities, past conditioning creating false beliefs about ourselves and others, and past confusion leaving us feeling like we are not deserving of the truth.

We walk out of childhood braced for battle like untrained warriors with no clear enemy in sight. Until we clear out the things we falsely believe to be true about ourselves and others it is very hard to acknowledge what our emotions bring to the table on a daily basis. Paying attention to ourselves in healthy ways (non-egotistic or self-serving) is the road we all seek but the past is what keeps the ego striving to misguide us. But when you keep the air clear around you, when you can speak openly, honestly from your heart and resolve things with others then peace within accompanies you on your path.

That clear air blowing in the calm of peace is what solidified my ability to ditch the avoidant coping and recognize food for the benefits it provides my body. Once I kicked all sources of anxiety to the curb and learned the tools to manage my feelings properly it was easy. Refocusing things internally changed my entire perspective of the world around me and what life was about. But that moment in the shower reminded me of one of the most important lessons I've learned which is the lesson of how little I know.

Almost before I started on this path I wanted to be finished. The role I'd taken on of efficiency expert somewhere in the past pushed me to be in a hurry. I could have let it go and chalked it up as an innate part of my personality. But that crucial moment where I questioned the professional I'd entrusted my growth with opened my mind to a new way of thinking about myself. I am ever evolving. The truth of who I was to become was lost decades ago but the beauty of who I can become now unfolds daily.

I understand it's so much easier to say there is nothing in your past that haunts you. But in my experience working with both clients and friends, this is where the core root is, each and every time. I keep a growing list: whether it's been recognizing the dysfunction of an alcoholic parent, an over-the-top caregiver, a perfectionist mother who caused anger in her daughter whenever she thought someone made her look bad, a marriage that had gone on for years that therapy didn't dislodge or something as simple as a need for coffee only at work, finding the answer in childhood has been the case for each and every one I've spoken with. I firmly believe the truth is here for us all if we can open our minds to the idea that it's possible.

CHAPTER 39: JOY IS FOUND IN THE TRUTH

Consciousness is the keeper of inner peace and sustainable happiness.

My visits with Sean had gone on in spurts over the course of the years, sometimes out of frustration, once in a while there may have been a reprieve, or occasionally I worked it out on my own. On one of my later visits, I had gone into the meeting with some sort of anger or resentment because of the all-or-nothing approach I took with certain things. Not all things, mainly food and drink, beer specifically. Gradually, I'd removed the epic battles in the freezer section with the sugary crap. Eventually, I'd been able to keep a few snacks in the house. Finally, I could redirect my favorites to be the healthiest foods. All because I took the time to break down the core root cause every time I had an issue or trigger. I tried many other things alongside this. For a while I kept a spreadsheet on what I ate, what I weigh and how the food had made me feel physically. But the one and only thing I found that actually healed me was finding the core root of the triggers. Doing the work with each to understand, process and release the repressed and trapped emotional pain or fear that anchored my dysfunctional behavior to it.

This time I was having trouble with beer. There was no stopping by to meet a friend for one beer, I couldn't put a cap on it if you will excuse the pun. So, under I went but before I even got to the usual door I saw a black strip to the right and a cloudy strip to the left. I felt that the cloudy strip wanted to overtake the black strip. In our discussion before my hypothesis Sean had asked me why I didn't feel allowed to enjoy myself, which we decided was something my dad projected onto me consistently with his actions.

As I tried to make sense of the strips of color and cloudiness Sean asked more about what sorts of things my dad had liked. I said that my dad didn't enjoy life, (other than distractions like horse racing, and his worship of rationing sweets) but he had talked a lot about enjoying it before. Like he had one life he enjoyed before I was born. And one he despised afterwards. I said he resented me. Sean said he was not resentful of me but more so of my mother for taking away his freedom.

And then it all made sense, it wasn't me, any soul could have found themselves there and been conditioned in the same way from that projected resentment. Unhappy people just throw unhappiness onto others without concern.

And then I knew. I was allowed to enjoy myself, in whatever ways I wanted. This visit had not taken me to my own deeply hidden inner pain as so many had before. We'd rung that pain dry. Instead, this was about the messaging my dad had projected onto my own belief system. His resentment had settled over me like a dark cloud. With this visit, it lifted.

In two months, it will have been ten years since the day I nearly died. Almost all of this time has been spent away from the workplace and buried deep in thought, reflection, and research. With Sean's brilliant guidance, deep into the layers of my subconscious and Tom's patient coaching along with the support of many dear friends and the love of my son, I found my way to a place of honest self-love.

It began with acceptance. I had to learn to be ok with who I was and who I had been. I had to look at my overweight body and tell myself, that's ok and thank you. Thank you for carrying the burdens of my emotions when I was not prepared or taught to do so. I had to accept that I had not been the best mom for my son or the best wife or girlfriend or even the best friend a lot of the time. And that I had been a person who'd spoken her mind in ways that had been painful to other people because I had been so wrong about all the things I had been so certain of.

And then I had to let myself off the hook for all of that because it wasn't my fault that I'd been dragging around all of the deeply hidden pain, frustration, fear, confusion, and messaging. All of which had created all of the walls which kept me from a connection with myself and others on a deeper emotional level with empathy and kindness. And make no mistake, beating yourself up is not kind.

It took me almost two years to finish reading the book *The Untethered Soul* which coincided with my last visits with Sean. It was then I could step fully into my own truth, uncloaked, and unburdened by my past for the first time. I stepped into the truth about self-love. It had been impossible for me to love me for me as the person I had been because there were too many beliefs about myself that were negative and false. I was hiding and lashing out in the pain I carried. But as we cleared that by going backwards, I was able to see myself going forward. I saw the little girl I had to drag out of hiding. I saw a mom who opened her heart and loved to the depth of her being. I saw a woman who's heart had finally come alive once she connected with the depth of her own soul. But mostly I saw a woman who wanted to do better with her relationships, starting with herself.

I don't know how to bring the balance I've found into all my relationships, but I do share it with those who have picked up their own emotional baggage and have begun unpacking. It doesn't seem to be enough to just become aware of the bags and even to open them up to see who helped you pack them. That doesn't quite finish the work to be fully emotionally self-aware. We have to unpack them piece by piece and empty the case until we see there is nothing left inside. Or at least that was what was needed for me to fully release my addiction and find peace and freedom. Because, just as we can identify a feeling and process it, if that feeling is not released it stays put right there waiting for its day in the light, causing anxiety.

Emotions are just emotions, nothing other than a feeling. But, as kids, many if not all of us were taught to ignore our feelings rather than manage them properly. They are meant to be fleeting little indicators along the path that we grab for a second, appreciate their messages and let them fly back off into the open. Many of us on this planet have a surplus of them, a stockade in reserve, waiting desperately to escape, getting crushed under the weight as more are left unattended each day. They scream out to us with things they hope we'll pay attention to. For me it was a weight issue because of the food addiction that I used as avoidant coping. We crave more internally but just continue using the external to placate us. Our souls deeply desire the balance of inner peace and a conscious lifestyle.

Love seeks us. I believe we can find shared love with others, deep connections that are not one sided or codependent, but are in balance...once we find that in our relationship with ourselves. Just as finding acceptance and understanding for others is the most natural thing once you find it for yourself.

While I didn't openly choose this path or necessarily welcome the strangest elements it threw at me, it was the dogged pursuit in breaking my own dysfunctional behavior that helped my mind stay open to what I could learn from it all. It was exactly that open-minded curiosity that presented all of the possibilities I may have otherwise thrown out as impossible.

I finally made peace with food. I am released from the cage that once bound me. I won the battle because I opened my mind up to possibilities that seemed too impossible to even consider. How can childhood be a problem if you don't remember it being one...sadly it can and is for everyone.

Every scrap of old pain has been scraped out of my subconscious and I am able to make conscious choices, no longer needing the dysfunctional avoidant coping methods I clung to in the past. By unearthing the deeply rooted pain from childhood I removed everything that sent me out of control. I now consciously choose the path to weight loss instead of feeling like it's something I need to do but can't quite make it happen because of the baggage in my subconscious. I am now free to make the healthy choices for myself that I wanted all along.

It can be easy to believe that we are capable of making healthy choices for ourselves, but self-sabotage removes our ability to choose self-care when our subconscious is heavily burdened. Putting myself in the position to finally have a choice was the important part.

For the first time in my life, I feel balanced, but I also know I have a long way to go. I've only just skimmed the surface of what there is to learn.

And so far I've lost 30 pounds.

CHAPTER40: LOOKING FORWARD

Maybe authentic self is just another name for our soul.

I am hopeful that humanity will catch up with nature and spirit. And it does seem that both nature and spirit are conspiring to make that happen these days, if only we humans would hear their messages. If I hadn't been shoved down this path I'm not sure I would have given things like that much thought, but the good news is, a lot of other people are opening up to new awareness.

Perhaps we are all born with our soul exposed only to spend our lives undoing the damage caused by humanity. Maybe mindfulness is another word for emotional self-awareness or consciousness. It could be that many addictions are more about the pain from the past than an incurable disease, and maybe the same can be said of some disorders. I just read an article proposing that personalities are perhaps not set in stone as once thought to be. Soon, many more people could find themselves confronting intense soul connections, taking them into deep personal introspection. Looking inward is a spiritual journey that can lead to universal consciousness where staying on a materialistic hamster wheel can keep you trapped in unconsciousness. Perhaps balance lies in the middle of understanding both, but the answers are always within us. **Inner peace doesn't seek external distractions.**

For me it was a conditioned pattern of panic that pulled me out of consciousness and into the freezer section at the grocery store. By the grace of it all, that is no longer the case. I've found that when you walk in the purpose of kindness you will find peace and the most important place to find that is from within. Perfection is found in the acceptance of yourself just as you are in each moment because light can't shine without darkness.

For those of you who think there is nothing in your past holding you back I ask this, is anything holding you back? Is there anything you want to change in or about your life? If the answer is yes then I'm 99.9% certain that it comes from something in your childhood.

I got lucky. I had no clue what I was doing or what I needed to do. If I'd not had the first meeting with Sean and revisited my stuffed avocado incident I wouldn't have given my childhood any more thought than I had before I met him. This is how good the subconscious is at hiding it all away from us. It's so good, it's like it's not even there.

Our subconscious wants to protect us so it creates a disassociation between ourselves and our bodies so we can continue using food/alcohol/smoke, etc. to cope. And it's hella good at hiding our truths from us which means you have to be that much more committed to finding it. The ability to emotionally connect with ourselves has the single largest impact on how we manage our lives...and is sadly what we seem to pay the least attention to.

The single most important relationship you will ever have is the one you have with yourself. That relationship takes work. It requires you know who you are, what you like, what you want and how your life became what it is.

Of the thousands of books, blogs, journals, and posts I've read here are a few that cover a lot of ground.

The Conscious Parent by Dr. Shefali Tsabary.

There Are No Accidents: Synchronicity and the Stories of Our Lives by Robert H. Hopcke.

The Untethered Soul, the Journey Beyond Yourself by Michael A. Singer.

And of course, Brene Brown.

IN GRATITUDE

There are some very specific people that made it possible for me to make it through all this and come out where I have.

For my son, who's carried the burden of my past until it's nearly broken him – I explicitly release you from that burden with gratitude that exceeds even my own existence and the depth of unconditional love and respect bursting from my heart with each beat.

For Tom, my coach and mentor who became my friend the moment he stepped through the door and has continued to ride the tides of life with me in a way that I'm not sure anyone else could have.

For Sean, who opened the door to my soul and stood patiently as I crept my way through each and every crevice of the darkness of my past and into the light of freedom.

For Kevin who held his door as wide open as his arms in an eternal embrace of friendship like the family I'd wished had been mine at birth.

For Brad and Tiffany whose family has brought beauty into my life in all ways. Their kind acceptance, welcoming spirits and soulful openness has made the journey one filled with love and unforgettable memories.

For Nita my ride or die, that part!

For Remy my friend, confidant, and travel buddy through all kinds of terrain.

For Chuck who was my rock star reading ninja and an all-time solid friend no matter what, when where, how, or why.

For Koungie an uncommonly amazing friend who I wouldn't be the same without. Thank you for showing me I wasn't really a fat kid!

For Jolyne who opened her home to me during the worst days of my life and did all she could to make things better. Thank you friend.

For Eric who helped guide me in the telling of my story.

For Anshu and Nana who walked the path of craziness as my witnesses, confidants, and beautiful soul connections.

For Vincent and Herbert who've been meant to be a part of this journey from the start.

For Catherine who's heard it all and shows up no matter

what.

For those who have come before, such as Emma and her mom who have chosen to release me I wish you all only the best. I wish I could take whatever made you leave me behind and heal it but maybe a season was all we were meant to have.

And all the men of past relationships who have each touched my heart in ways I can only now appreciate. My deeply sincere apologies for the old me.

And lastly for Drew who has been an amazing part of my life for twenty years when I needed rescuing the most. Hopefully you can find acceptance in the me who no longer needs that.

Some names have been changed in the writing of this book for privacy. xoxo